proclamation 2

Aids for Interpreting the Lessons of the Church Year

holy week

Richard L. Jeske
and
Browne Barr

series a

editors: Elizabeth Achtemeier · Gerhard Krodel · Charles P. Price

FORTRESS PRESS PHILADELPHIA

Unless otherwise noted, biblical quotations are in the author's own translation. Biblical quotations from the Revised Standard Version of the Bible, copyrighted 1946, 1952, © 1971, 1973 by the Division of Christian Education of the National Council of the Churches of Christ in the U.S.A., are used by permission.

The quotations on pp. 32 and 35 from *The Eighth Day* by Thornton Wilder, Harper & Row, Publishers, Inc., copyright © 1967 by The Union & New Haven Trust Company, are reprinted by special permission.

Library of Congress Cataloging in Publication Data (Revised)

Main entry under title:

Proclamation 2.

Consists of 24 volumes in 3 series designated A, B, and C which correspond to the cycles of the three year lectionary plus 4 volumes covering the lesser festivals. Each series contains 8 basic volumes with the following titles: Advent-Christmas, Epiphany, Lent, Holy Week, Easter, Pentecost 1, Pentecost 2, and Pentecost 3.

CONTENTS: [etc.]—Series C: [1] Fuller, R. H. Advent-Christmas. [2] Pervo, R. I. and Carl III, W. J. Epiphany.—Thulin, R. L. et al. The lesser festivals. 4 v.

1. Bible—Homiletical use. 2. Bible—Liturgical lessons, English.

[BS534.5.P76] 251 79-7377

ISBN 0-8006-4079-9 (ser. C, v. 1)

8272E80 Printed in the United States of America 1-4094

Contents

Editor's Foreword

On his celebrated trip to the Orient, Marco Polo was taken before the greatly feared conqueror Genghis Khan. Marco Polo could find nothing better to do on that occasion than to relate the story of Jesus, simply as written in the Gospels. It is said that as Marco Polo came to the events of Holy Week and described Jesus' betrayal, trial, scourging, and crucifixion, the Turk became more and more engrossed in the narrative and increasingly tense. After Marco Polo pronounced the words "He bowed his head and gave up the ghost," Genghis Khan could no longer contain himself. He gave a loud cry and interrupted. "What did the Christians' God do then? Did he send his thousands of legions from heaven to smite and destroy those who had so treated his Son?"

Polo's answer plainly failed to satisfy Genghis Khan. The Turk remained unconverted. But that he was so completely caught up in the Gospel narrative and deeply moved by the story of Holy Week will come as no surprise to anyone who has heard it in its entirety during the liturgies of this most central and solemn week of the Christian year. Though the best known of all stories, it never grows stale, but renews its strength year after year.

After the great fifty days from Easter to Pentecost, Holy Week was the next part of the Christian year to be elaborated. Already in the second century there was some celebration of the Friday before Pascha, since every Friday was a commemoration of the cross. Good Friday has its roots in this observance. The celebration of the rest of Holy Week was worked out by Cyril of Jerusalem in the fourth century.

The new ecumenical lectionary on which these proclamation aids are based supplies a new context to this most ancient of readings, a new set of First and Second Lessons to illuminate the Lord's passion. New opportunities for preaching open up. The exegetical and homiletical aids contained in this volume are presented in the hope that they will contribute to a deeper understanding of these texts and so to a more searching examination of the mighty acts of God for us and for our salvation. Yet once more the proclamation of the gospel at this season may be renewed.

The exegetical section of this volume was written by Richard L.

Jeske, Professor of New Testament at the Lutheran Theological Seminary in Philadelphia. He is the author of numerous articles in *Dialog* and *Currents in Theology and Mission,* and he is book editor of *Dialog*.

The homiletical commentary was prepared by Browne Barr, who after a distinguished career at Yale as Professor of Homiletics and pastor at Berkeley is now serving as Dean of the San Francisco Theological Seminary in San Anselmo. He is author of *The Well Church Book* and *Parish Back Talk* (The Lyman Beecher Lectures, 1963).

Alexandria, Va. CHARLES P. PRICE

Sunday of the Passion
Palm Sunday

Lutheran	Roman Catholic	Episcopal	Pres/UCC/Chr	Meth/COCU
Isa. 50:4–9a	Isa. 50:4–7	Isa. 45:21–25 or Isa. 52:13—53:12	Isa. 50:4–7	Isa. 50:4–9a
Phil. 2:5–11	Phil. 2:6–11	Phil. 2:5–11	Phil. 2:5–11	Phil. 2:5–11
Matt. 26:1—27:66 or Matt. 27:11–54	Matt. 26:14—27:66 or Matt. 27:11–54	Matt. (26:36–75) 27:1–54 (55–66)	Matt. 21:1–11	Matt. 26:14—27:66

EXEGESIS

During Holy Week the First Lessons include the four songs of the servant of Yahweh: Isa. 42:1–4 (Monday); 49:1–6 (Tuesday); 50:4–9 (Sunday and Wednesday), and 52:13—52:12 (Good Friday). In 1892 Bernard Duhm detected the independence of these songs from their immediate context. His view has prevailed, although there is widely divergent opinion concerning the origin and interpretation of the songs. A brief summary of research on the figure of the servant is given in *Second Isaiah* by John L. McKenzie in the Anchor Bible, pp. xliii–lv. It cannot be said with certainty that any of the songs originally presupposed any of the others, even though the responses following each song do show knowledge of the other songs. The interpreter may therefore approach each one by itself, but for our purposes here the reader is urged to review the present exegesis of all four songs together. The Holy Week lectionary begins with the third song, which is repeated on Wednesday.

First Lesson: Isa. 50:4–9a. The speaker is the servant, who in the midst of shame and ridicule is able to withstand the hostility directed to him because of what Yahweh has done for him. His ministry has brought him adversity and insult, but his strength to endure is provided by God's own leading. That is the good news of this song: "Yahweh has given" and "Yahweh wakens" (v. 4); "Yahweh has opened" (v. 5) and "Yahweh helps" (vv. 7 and 9); "he vindicates" (v. 8). On his own the servant is vulnerable, but with Yahweh at his side no adversary can prevail. The precise experiences of the servant seem to be more those of shame and insult than physical suffering.

Such a description may well allude to the general experiences of Israelite apostasy in exile or elsewhere, and in that case this song is a prophetic song of trust and a call to steadfast endurance.

But in order to be a spokesman for Yahweh, the servant must first be a listener: "The Lord Yahweh has given me a disciple's tongue, that I may know how to feed the weary" (v. 4). In order *to feed* (RSV "to sustain with a word"; the Hebrew word is obscure) the weary, the servant must first be fed. The word for "disciple" here is used rarely in the OT; it designates the student who commits his teacher's words to memory; his "tongue" repeats faithfully what he has learned. The servant does not come by his prophetic wisdom naturally: each day Yahweh wakens and opens his ear to hear the word which sustains him and the others to whom he ministers. He is not confounded by his challengers, because of Yahweh's help to him (v. 7).

Vv. 8–9a use the language of the lawcourts, but that does not mean the servant is at home there; elsewhere in the OT (cf. Job 13:18; 23:4) such language is used to express confidence in God. St. Paul's use of it in Rom. 8:33, with direct reference to our text, depicts Jesus as the advocate before God, the justifying Judge. Both Paul and the servant know that they do not stand alone, that no adversary (cf. Rom. 8:35) can overcome the one whose vindication comes from God. That is the message which sustains and feeds the weary.

Second Lesson: Phil. 2:5–11. The preacher has several options when approaching the exegesis of this passage as a sermon text: (1) as a pre-Pauline hymn with its own theological themes apart from its immediate context; (2) as an example of a Pauline adjustment (on the strength of his addition to the hymn of the last phrase of v. 8) to a theology which sounds rather removed from the world in which we live; (3) as an element within the context of the letter, relating to Paul's immediate concerns; (4) all of the above.

Generally, NT scholarship refers to vv. 6–11 as the "Christ hymn," a pre-Pauline Christian hymn using an ancient theme of the descent and ascent of the heavenly Redeemer. It is not originally a Christian theme, but its adaptation for Christian use emphasized various subthemes which have become focal points in christological debate throughout subsequent centuries: the identification of the heavenly Redeemer with Jesus of Nazareth, his preexistence in the form of God (*morphē* = "form," not nature), his "emptying" (*kenosis*) of himself, his obedience, his exaltation. None of these are typically Pauline themes. This fact, along with vocabulary and the metric structure of the passage, has suggested its independent nature as a hymn used in early Christian worship.

Paul's addition to the hymn expresses a certain caution about its content. The addition is the final phrase of v. 8, "even death on a cross," detectable because it is the *fourth* line in the verse, breaking the consistent pattern of *three* lines in each verse (or in each strophe) of the hymn. Of course, the theology of the final phrase in v. 8 is especially Pauline and insists that the event of salvation is not something which is played out on an otherworldly stage. The Redeemer's self-emptying obedience takes place in Jesus' death on the cross, an event in the history of this world. The divine form is set aside for that of the Crucified Servant, so that God can take it from there (v. 9).

The Pauline adjustment allows the hymn to serve its context more precisely. "God is at work among you" (v. 13), so therefore let that work surface in each of you (v. 12). "Do nothing from selfishness or conceit, but in humility count others better than yourselves. Let each of you look not only to his own interest, but also to the interest of others" (vv. 3–4). That will happen if you allow "that thinking to be among you which is also in Messiah Jesus" (v. 5). The admonition toward humility becomes moralistic if it is isolated from God's work in Messiah Jesus and now in us. The gospel, especially for Paul, is that it is precisely the Crucified Servant Jesus whom God has exalted and appointed as the object of all worship and confession (vv. 10–11). If God's Messiah is the Crucified, where then can our selfishness, conceit, and grasping be? If God is at work among us, then our thinking about each other will be determined by his work in the Crucified.

The personal pronoun in v. 5 (*en hymin* = "among you," also in v. 13) rules out a sense of a privatistic moralism in the admonition toward humility. God's work builds relationships, and therefore community; it is not a work "*within* me" but rather a work "*among* us." That is evident also in the conclusion of the hymn, where allusion is made to Isa. 45:23, a passage Paul uses in Rom. 14:11. Christians are members of a community for whom God has provided a means of building toward each other: the vindication of the Servant-Messiah who emptied himself and became obedient unto death.

Gospel: Matt. 26:1—27:66. The prelude to the Matthean passion narrative is Jesus' entry into Jerusalem (Matt. 21:1–9), in which Matthew sees the fulfillment of Zech. 9:9 and Isa. 62:11:

> Tell the daughter of Zion,
> Behold, your king is coming to you,
> humble, and mounted on an ass,
> and on a colt, the foal of an ass.
> (21:5 RSV)

The two animals mentioned in the prophecy are obtained in Matthew's account simply by the statement "The Lord has need of them." The story is paralleled at the beginning of the passion narrative by the report of the obtaining of a room for the Last Supper (Matt. 26:17–19). The disciples are sent to a certain man in the city to say that the Lord needs his house (Mark and Luke: "upper room"): "The Teacher says, My time *(kairos)* is at hand; I will keep the passover at your house with my disciples" (26:18 RSV). In both stories the initiative is with Jesus, as Teacher, Lord, and King.

J. S. Bach has caught the connection between the stories in the opening chorus of his *St. Matthew Passion:*

> Come, you daughters, share my mourning;
> Look! On whom? The Bridegroom Christ.
> See him! How? A Lamb unblemished.
> See it! What? His patient love.
> Look! Look where? On our offense.
> Look on him. For love of us
> He himself his cross is bearing.

The scene depicted in the chorus is not one of sentimental mourning or of self-flagellation seeking an earned reward. It is not a portrayal of an unfortunate rabbi caught up in an ill-fated series of mob actions and kangaroo courts. At every step, as in Matthew, Jesus is in control of both himself and the situation far more than his captors are.

Matthew makes a number of prominent additions to Mark's account of the passion: Judas's payoff of thirty pieces of silver; the cup at the Last Supper as Jesus' blood of the covenant poured out "for the forgiveness of sins"; Jesus' rebuke of unnamed disciple for his swordplay in Gethsemane; Judas's death; Pilate's wife's dream; Pilate's hand washing; the opening of the tombs and the raising of many bodies of the saints at Jesus' death; Joseph of Arimathea as a disciple; the guard set at Jesus' tomb.

As Jack Dean Kingsbury has shown in *Matthew: Structure, Christology, Kingdom* (Philadelphia: Fortress Press, 1975), it is precisely as the Son of God that Matthew's Jesus is condemned by the Sanhedrin (26:63–64), mocked by the onlookers and the robbers who were crucified with him (27:39–44), and then in turn confessed by the soldiers (27:54) who understand the epiphany as it is accompanied by the supernatural portents (27:51–53). This is Jesus' *kairos* (26:18), and he accomplishes it in willing obedience and trust as God's Son. Therefore, Matthew does not report, as does Mark, that Jesus prays that his *hour* pass from him (cf. the absence of Mark 14:35 in

Matthew). For Matthew that is not the intent of the prayer. By softening the direct request in Mark 14:36, the emphasis falls rather on Jesus' obedience to his Father: "nevertheless not as I will, but as thou wilt" (26:39 RSV).

Jesus' response to Judas's betrayal kiss lacks the question mark in the Greek texts and is not easy to decipher. It could be exclamatory: "My friend, for what a purpose you have come!" It could be imperative: "My friend, get on with that for which you have come!" The earlier prediction of the betrayal at the Last Supper shows that Judas's action can be no surprise to Jesus, and therefore Jesus' response to Judas's kiss appears as a challenge to Judas to unravel the inner turmoil which brought him to such duplicitous action. Once again, the Betrayed is sovereign to the betrayer.

In the next scene (26:51–54) it is the Captive who speaks in freedom. He will not condone violent action, nor be party to it. He will not request an army of angels to deliver him from this hour, for his *kairos* has come in fulfillment of the Scriptures: the Son is here to carry out the will of his Father. That Jesus did not prepare his disciples for armed confrontation is shown by the spontaneous thrust of a single swordsman (John 18:10 identifies him as Peter); nor are his fleeing disciples pursued and captured as Zealotic revolutionaries. Jesus' rebuke of the sword-wielding disciple is a rejection of all attempts to secure God's future by our own designs. V. 52b is to be used not as a proof text for the validity of capital punishment but rather as a proverbial admonition of those whose vision is limited by their unwillingness to seek beyond the horizon of their own mortal power. The Captive here speaks in eschatological freedom.

The story of the death of Judas (Matt. 27:3–10) presupposes the earlier account that Judas was paid for his action, and it may represent the development of an earlier tradition reflected in Acts 1:18–19. However, the fulfillment-of-Scripture motif is applied in Acts to the burial of Judas and in Matthew 27 to the purchase of the field by the chief priests. Matthew's OT quotation obviously recalls Zech. 11:12–13, but his introductory reference to Jeremiah shows that he has combined Jeremiah's visit to the potter (Jer. 18:1ff.) and his purchase of land from his cousin (32:6–9; LXX 39:6–9) with the Zechariah passage to explain the riddle of Judas not as a deviation from but as a part of the events of sacred history.

Matthew (27:1) and John (11:47–53) state that the Sanhedrin had determined Jesus' fate before the trial began, but only John (18:3, 12) reports Roman complicity in the arrest of Jesus in the garden. Matthew stresses the culpability of the Jewish leadership throughout by paying more attention to the proceedings of the Jewish court, without mentioning (as in John 18:31) that the Sanhedrin did not have the power to inflict the death penalty. Whereas Luke reports Pilate's express declaration of the innocence of Jesus, Matthew emphasizes that judgment by two dramatic scenes: (1) Pilate's wife's report of her dream (27:19), and (2) Pilate's hand washing (27:24), leaving the Jews solely responsible for the outcome. The result is escalated with the chilling cry "His blood be on us and our children!"

To avoid the anti-Semitic perversions which have built upon that passage to heap insult and injury on Jewish people down to the present time, a great deal of care and insight must be brought to its public reading and interpretation. If Matthew, writing to Jewish readers from his perspective as a Jewish Christian, intends to confront his readers with the gravity of the rejection of Messiah—as he does elsewhere (cf. 21:43)—his only concern is Israel's relationship with God and not with other races. Matthew does not pen 27:25 in order to justify gentile evil toward his people. The shepherds of gentile flocks today do indeed have a ministry to avoid vilification of Jews, especially when the passion narrative is read. (Cf. the final exegetical comments for Good Friday.)

Jesus' silence before Pilate is emphasized in Matthew: "He gave them [that is, the governor, priest, and elders] no answer, not even to a single charge" (27:14 RSV). The latter phrase is an addition of Matthew's. There is no lengthy discussion between Jesus and Pilate as in John 18:33ff. As he had replied to the high priest's question before the Sanhedrin (26:63–64), Jesus answers Pilate's query whether he were king of the Jews: "You have said so" (27:11). "The words are yours" is both *more and less* than affirmative: *more,* because the claim is not solely on the lips of the accused, and must therefore be dealt with by the accuser; *less,* because Jesus and his person are not under judgment here, but his accusers are. Therefore, the majestic silence of Jesus in Matthew suggests that he is controlled by nothing other than obedience to his Father. All this is his *kairos*.

The eschatological power of Jesus' death is underscored by Matthew's addition of significant signs to Mark's report of the tearing of the temple curtain (Matt. 27:51–53). Jesus' death provides new and free access to God's presence, a theme sounded in Heb. 6:19; 9:12; 10:19–22. The death of Jesus has broken the power of death, and therefore it must remain at the center of Christian proclamation. The significance of such portents, long expected to accompany the great apocalyptic Day of the Lord, is that Jesus' death is the *kairos* (Matt. 26:18), the hour (26:55), the cup (26:39), the eschatological deed of God. And therefore the response of the soldiers (as "neutral" observers) is a believing one: "Truly this was the Son of God."*

HOMILETICAL INTERPRETATION

The Gospel for this Sunday is very long. It is very heavy. It could be titled "The Story of the Death of Jesus." The contemporary preacher may be freed to do his or her work most effectively on this Sunday and throughout this Holy Week if he or she relies upon the story, rests in it, works out from it, learns from it, and allows it to proclaim Christ. The preacher may discern in the story not only the message but the method offered there to the preacher for preaching it. The drama which these two chapters unfold can provide the framework for the sermon, or there are many smaller dramas within the whole which could be handled the same way. The preacher could select them from the "prominent additions to Mark's account" noted by the exegesis. Indeed, such incidents could provide the framework for a series of Holy Week sermons enriched by one or more of the suggested lessons. It is important that the preacher discover not only the framework in the narrative but also the movement, the development, the suspense. That is where vitality is in a sermon, just as in a lesser story.

At other seasons of the Christian year we are confronted with other "chapters," as it were, in the story of Jesus. This chapter, this season, however, makes it difficult for the responsible preacher to avoid the injunction to preach "Christ and him crucified." That part of the story, "The Death of Jesus," is what is reenacted in the church during the week, and the preaching is a primary part of that reenactment. So the theme for the week is given. We do not choose it. But alas, frequently it is so declared and preached that it simply lays another load upon an already burdened humanity and in no way prepares the hearers to receive the liberating Gift which is the end and purpose of the story. So Easter is the larger implicit context, and as it cannot be appropriated without the pain of Holy Week, so also that pain is a searing sortie against the lonely sky without the hint of the Easter dawn in the foreground.

The three lessons which the exegesis has helped open up for us have variations of one common, dominant theme which can be drawn on to illumine and clarify the story. In the Isaiah passage the speaker

*Grammatically, the definite article in the phrase *the* Son of God should be retained, since in NT Greek definite predicate nouns which precede the verb usually lack the article. Theologically, Matthew (and also Mark 15:39) certainly understands the centurion's remark as a fully Christian confession of faith; anything less weakens the impact of the story.

is "the servant." We are told that he has been ridiculed and that his ministry has brought him "adversity and insult." And although the Gospel makes clear at every step that "Jesus is in control of both himself and the situation far more than his captors are," the story still moves inexorably to the crucifixion. The Philippians text is a "Christ hymn" singing the praise of One who did not think equality with God something to be grasped but emptied himself taking a slave's form. In each instance there is a particular kind of action: voluntary suffering on behalf of others. It is dim but nonetheless present in the Isaiah lesson. It is the thundering inescapable *action* in the Gospel. It is the center of the vigorous reflection and praise and instruction in the Philippians lesson.

We don't like stories which drag. We like to have them move along. We like *action*. However, the preacher may want to suggest that action is of concern and interest because it is how we know *persons*. Vernard Eller in an excellent little book for lay people and ministers alike, *His End Up* (Nashville: Abingdon Press, 1969), reminds us that "a person is 'actions,' not 'stuff.' Right here," he writes (pp. 46, 49),

> is quite a divergence from the customary methods of getting at God; most theology would define God in terms of his "being," essence, substance, inner nature, "stuff." What is he made out of?—to put it crudely. But even if we would take for granted that some sort of God-stuff lies behind what we identify as God-actions, how would you propose that we go about getting at it? . . .
>
> The interest of scientists has tended more and more to shift away from the attempt to discover *what* things are and to be content with discovering *how* they operate. And we submit that such an approach to "person" will both open new possibilities of understanding and at the same time get us to the most fundamental truth about persons.

So we know the essence of a person in his or her actions. In fact, we identify people that way. A little boy was visiting his grandmother in California and almost wore her out with his vigorous activity. One night when they were both sound asleep there was a pretty good earthquake. The grandmother was awakened by the shaking and called out, "Billy! Billy!" To which came a response, "Honest, Grandma, I didn't do it." So! By actions we know persons. That earthquake was like Billy to a grandmother who ordinarily lived a peaceful, quiet, orderly life.

By our actions we are revealed. Eller tells the story of an American soldier who has written his wife about the seven men with whom he has developed a deep relationship in an isolated and dangerous post. When his birthday rolls around, a package is delivered to him from the

States. When he opens it, he discovers not one gift but eight. One for him and one for each of his new friends. He looks at the opened package and exclaims, "There's my wife for you!" She was revealed there by her action. That was the kind of thing she would do.

So with the "suffering theme" in these three lessons: "There's our God for you!" The price love will pay for the beloved, not to exalt itself but to save the other. Whenever that kind of love breaks out in human life, there is *the* Christ. It was explicit in Jesus and in human form. As we preachers work to allow "The Story of the Death of Jesus" to tell itself, we shall need to discover human, personal, warm, real ways to declare the divine Person revealed in the central action, the self-giving love.

The exegesis lifts up another motif which recurs again and again in all three of these lessons: *conflict*. The preacher must draw out one or two instances of it, but they seem almost endless: in Isaiah, insult and challenge and a great adversary; in Philippians, inner conflict and encouragement not to give in to self-interest and the dangers of pride; in Matthew, Judas, Caiaphas, Peter, Pilate, and the man of Cyrene—all are centers of conflict of one sort or another. The preacher who studies these conflicts with an eye to the conflicts which are besetting his or her congregation will find new openings for telling the story. It often introduces a welcome note of reality if the preacher scans the newspaper, not overlooking the want ads and the society column and the sports page, for hints of conflict—from world disorder to domestic strife—faced by every congregation.

Palm Sunday may be an appropriate time to reflect on conflict, for the picture of that day carried around by many ordinary Christians is the picture of a false celebration—Peace, peace, when there was no peace. If the preacher will follow these lessons, it will become clear that Christian peace is not the absence of conflict, that conflict in itself is not evil but can be creative and energizing. Indeed, Professor John Macquarrie describes the dynamics of Christian peace in terms of conflict. "Conflict," he claims, "must be included within wholeness. A wholeness which does not include conflict is a frozen condition, a kind of death lacking dynamism and the possibility of new development" (*The Concept of Peace* [New York: Harper & Row, Publishers, 1973], p. 34).

Palm Sunday and Holy Week may well be introduced by considering the problem our contemporary culture has in dealing with the report that Jesus was "mounted on an ass, and on a colt, the foal of an ass." The exegesis refers to this "two-animal" prophecy. Professor Herman Waetjen suggests that one animal was the kingly beast, the coronation animal, and that the other was the beast of burden. "The Story of the Death of Jesus," the Holy Week story, makes clear which he chose.

Monday in Holy Week

Lutheran	Roman Catholic	Episcopal	Pres/UCC/Chr	Meth/COCU
Isa. 42:1–9	Isa. 42:1–7	Isa. 42:1–9	Isa. 50:4–10	Isa. 42:1–9
Heb. 9:11–15		Heb. 11:39—12:3	Heb. 9:11–15	Heb. 9:11–15
John 12:1–11	John 12:1–11	John 12:1–11 or Mark 14:3–9	Luke 19:41–48	John 12:1–11

EXEGESIS

First Lesson: Isa. 42:1–9. This pericope includes the first of the servant songs (vv. 1–4) along with the response to it (vv. 5–9). Two of the other three songs are followed by responses (49:7–13 and 50: 10–11), written very possibly by different authors. In the first song (vv. 1–4) the speaker is Yahweh, who presents his servant as the one upon whom he had decided. The Servant's qualifications for his commission are enumerated (vv. 2–4), but in terms of the spirit Yahweh has given him (v.1). His *charisma* comes from God's choosing:

> Behold my servant whom I uphold,
> my chosen one in whom I delight.
> I have set my spirit upon him;
> he will bring forth truth (*mišpāṭ*
> [lit., judgment, justice]) to the nations.

The verbal adjective "chosen" is a favorite of Second and Third Isaiah, used elsewhere in the OT of David, Israel, Zion, and of Israelites in the plural. The Septuagint translators use the word *eklektos* and explicitly apply it to Israel as the servant in this passage. In the NT the word *eklektos* is applied to the Christian community (1 Pet. 2:9 et al.), to a particular Christian (Rom. 16:13), and to the Messiah (Luke 23:35). Once again, as in our discussion of Isa. 50:4–9, we notice Paul's use of servant song language in Rom. 8:33: "Who shall bring accusation against the *eklektoi* of God?" In Isa. 42:1 the word identifies the servant as the object of Yahweh's special decision, chosen for a mission.

There is an intimate association between the servant's *mission* and Yahweh's *decision*, solidified by the phrase "I have set my spirit upon him." The wording "upon him" cautions us against any allusion to the inner, spiritualistic experience of the prophet here; Yahweh's spirit is "upon him," that is, *around* him and *over* him, as the creative spirit of God similarly hovered *over* the face of the waters in Gen. 1:2. Yahweh's creative spirit enables his servant to carry out his mission: he will bring truth to the nations.

The Hebrew word *mišpāṭ* is often translated "judgment" (KJV) or "justice" (RSV, NEB, TEV, NAB), but here it means much more than the English words can deliver. It has to do with the full scope of divine wisdom for all people and the world *in which they live*. It must be seen along with the word *torah* in v. 4: God's instruction for faith and life. It is God's truth—his saving message concerning the present and future of the world—which the servant is called to bring forth to the nations, and therefore God's creative spirit must always accompany him in his ministry. That spirit will equip him with the necessary qualifications for helping and restoring Yahweh's broken people:

> 2He will not cry out nor raise his voice:
>   he will not shout in the street.
> 3He will not crush the bruised reed;
>   he will not extinguish the wick burning dimly.
> Faithfully he will bring forth *mišpāṭ*.
> 4He will not burn dimly,
>   nor will he be bruised,
>   until he establishes *mišpāṭ* on the earth.
>   The coastlands are waiting for his *torah*.

In the contrast to the barking of other public officials, the servant will not harangue his listeners or force his authority on them (v. 2); nor will he be insensitive to the oppressed and the weak (v. 3). His demeanor is one of graceful and deliberate persuasion. He will not fail to persuade, for he is God's spokesman bringing *mišpāṭ* and *torah* to the nations, a servant to the broken and powerless (v. 3a).

These ideas are repeated and amplified in the response to the song in vv. 5–9. It begins with reference to the God who has created the world and its inhabitants and concludes with reference to the "new things" of the future which he has planned for them. Yahweh's words in vv. 6–9 describe the mission of the servant, v. 6 finding a later echo in words addressed to Cyrus in 45:1 and 48:15 and to Israel in 41:10.

Yahweh has given his servant as a "covenant for the people," a "light to the nations." The servant sent by God is God's personal guarantee to all people that they will not be lost in darkness. Through his servant God has provided for their salvation and that is why God has called him. Small wonder, then, that the NT writers apply the imagery used in Isaiah's servant song (1) *to Jesus* (Luke 2:30–32; Acts 26:23; John 1:5; 3:19; 8:12; 12:35–36; cf. Luke 4:16–21; Matt. 4:16; 26:28; 1 Cor. 11:25), and (2) *to the proclaimers of the gospel* (Matt. 5:14; Acts 13:47; 2 Cor. 3:6; 4:6).

The first of the servant songs declares that the scope of God's saving activity is not to be confined to one people but to all who inhabit the world that he has created. The evangelist Matthew (12:15–21) sees in Jesus the fulfillment of this song and concludes his Gospel with the command of the risen Jesus to his disciples to "make disciples of all nations." In this way the Christian church takes up the mission of the servant who under God's spirit proclaims God's truth and instruction, *mišpāṭ* and *torah*, for the salvation of all peoples. The question remains, Can the church, which assumes the servant's mission, also assume the servant's style (Isa. 42:2–4)?

Second Lesson: Heb. 11:39—12:3. This lesson is the conclusion of a section (chap. 11) which illustrates the form and character of Hebrews: it is a sermon, or a series of sermons, dressed up only slightly as a letter (13:22–25); in 13:22 it is called "a word of exhortation" *(logos tēs paraklēseōs)*. The "therefore" of 12:1 connects the exhortation to the foregoing and will encourage the interpreter to look over the immediate context of the lesson.

The great theme of chap. 11 is faith, and in 11:1 the writer defines what dimension of the concept he has in mind. For Paul the word faith generally refers to the dynamic channel by which the believer receives and responds to God's gift of salvation. In the pastoral Letters and Jude faith refers to belief in a body of doctrine or in the teaching about Jesus. Heb. 11:1 defines faith as "the reality of things hoped for, the conviction of things not seen." This definition enables the author's exclusively paraenetic use of it, never connecting it with key theological ideas or soteriological formulas (such as "faith in Jesus Christ"). This is apparent in the author's reference to Hab. 2:4 in Heb. 10:38, where faith has to do with the *quality of endurance in believing* (cf. Paul's use of Hab. 2:4 in Rom. 1:17 and Gal. 3:11).

If paraenesis (that is, pastoral admonition and encouragement) is the aim of the author, then what is there to say about the situation of his readers (or hearers)? While a precise answer is hard to give, Heb. 10:32–39 provides the closest hint of a creative milieu for our passage: the author's readers have experienced persecution after their conversion to Christianity (10:32) and have been subjected to public abuse (10:33) and looting (10:34), though not yet execution (12:4). Their immediate future looks predictably grim, and what they are experiencing is far from the promises of abundant life they had come to expect from the preaching they had heard. Whether the problem of the delay of the Parousia is at the heart of the crisis is difficult to tell, but it would not be impossible.

The author's definition of "faith" and the supporting concepts around it emphasize that God's promises are not *yet* fulfilled but that they will be for those who are "imitators of those who have faith and patience" (6:12). They need endurance (10:36; 12:1) so that they hold their original realization to the end (3:14), maintaining their confidence and pride in their hope (3:6). They are to hold fast the confession of their hope without wavering (10:23). That, in fact, is faith. The crisis is apostasy, falling away (3:12), brought about by the deceitfulness of sin (3:13), disobedience (3:18; 4:6, 11). The gravity of the crisis is met head-on in 6:4–7 and 10:26–27, which speak of the impossibility of restoration for those who have fallen away (cf. 12:17), passages which seem to be, as Luther wrote, "contrary to all the gospels and to St. Paul's epistles," disqualifying Hebrews to be put "on the same level with the apostolic epistles" (from "Prefaces to the New Testament," Luther's Works [Philadelphia: Fortress Press, 1960] 35:394–95).

So concerned with the crisis of apostasy in his church, the author asserts that faith is the steadfast maintaining of confident hope in the promises of God for the future of his people. The course of time has not brought that fulfillment, and in a period of oppression faith is always put to the test. The author's responsibility, then, is pastoral encouragement, and in chap. 11 his paraenesis takes the form of a review of the heroes of sacred history, for they too did not reach the final goal of God's eschatological promises during their lifetimes. Yet they "all died in faith, not having received what was promised, but having seen it and greeted it from afar, and having acknowledged that they were strangers and exiles on the earth" (11:13 RSV). The rhetorical device of formulaic repetition—"By faith Abel . . . ," "By faith Enoch . . . ," "By faith Noah . . . ," "By faith Abraham . . ."—holds the homily and its intention together. The author's readers are now one with them by their faith, "that apart from us they should not be made perfect" (11:40 RSV).

Their solidarity with us lies not only in the fact that the past heroes of faith did not attain the heavenly promises during their lifetimes, nor only in that they provide us with a great cloud of witnesses testifying that on earth there is no abiding city. Nor is their solidarity with us a *quality* of character—steadfast endurance—by which the sermon would drift into moralistic banalities. In our text the author has introduced something new; or rather, with Jesus *God* has introduced something eschatologically new and better (11:40). Therefore, Jesus is not just another link in the chain of heroic examples of faith: he seals the solidarity of those faith-full both before and after him. How is this done? A close look at 12:2 will indicate a structure which parallels the Christ hymn of Philippians 2: paraenesis and hymn.

Heb. 12:2		Phil. 2:5–11
a. looking to Jesus	—paraenesis—	a. allow that thinking to be among you which you have in Christ Jesus
b. who for the joy that was set before him	—exaltation—	b. who though he was in the form of God did not count equality with God something to be held onto
c. enduring the cross, despising the shame	—humiliation—	c. vv. 7–8: emptied self. . . . obedient unto death
d. and is seated at the right hand of God	—exaltation—	d. vv. 9–11

This hymn structure, evident also in Heb. 5:8–10, reinforces the point that Jesus is not just another link in the chain of faith heroes; he embraces them all. His preexistence makes him the archetype for the ancient witnesses before him, his incarnation and exaltation make him the prototype for those who follow him. In him is our solidarity with the faith heroes of the past: the preexistent Crucified and Exalted One. He is the pioneer and perfector of the faith *of us all,* both guarantor and guarantee of the promises of God's future, precisely in those moments when God's future seems so remote.

Gospel: Luke 19:41–48. Jesus' lament over Jerusalem in Luke 13:34–35 is the prelude to this pericope. The earlier lament is joined to the saying in 13:31–33 stating that "it cannot be that a prophet should perish away from Jerusalem" (RSV). A Q saying, 13:34–35 seems to presuppose some ministry in Jerusalem and therefore would fit better into the period after the entry into Jerusalem, as in Matt. 23:37–39. Luke, however, sees 13:35b as anticipatory of the acclamation of the crowds during the entry, and places it earlier in the journey toward the city. Luke also anticipates his own inclusion of the more precise details of the destruction of Jerusalem (now past for Luke) which are voiced in 19:43–44.

For the prophet of God Jerusalem is the place of enmity. Yet it is still the place of revelation, of God's visitation. It is the place where the message of God meets head-on the designs his people place on his future. The sending of his prophets to speak for him is God's gracious act of visitation (Wisd. of Sol. 4:15) to call his people to repentance, that is, to turning away from their agendas, away from their attempts to control God, and toward openness to his future.

Jesus was not the first prophet to lament the impending doom of the city. We recall Jeremiah's moving words,

> O that my head were waters,
> and my eyes a fountain of tears,
> that I might weep day and night
> for the slain of the daughter of my people!
> (9:1 RSV)

The prophet takes no pleasure in that which results from the rejection of his message, for his appearance is a sign of God's love for his people. That it is not recognized as such and not heeded is cause for his deep sorrow and grief. What future can there be for those who build their security on their own efforts?

Luke's redaction of this predictive lament into this context is striking in several ways. (1) The shout of the multitude of disciples in 19:38b, found only in Luke, forms a perfect antiphonal response to the angelic hymn of praise in 2:14 (so Raymond E. Brown, *Birth of the Messiah* [Garden City, N.Y.: Doubleday & Co., 1977], p. 427); but 19:11 indicates that the actual sentiments behind the acclamation are misguided, allowing 19:38b to serve as the connecting link for Jesus' statement in v. 42, "If only you knew today the things that are needed for peace!" (2) By placing the lament here Luke connects it with the disciples' own misunderstanding in 19:11; they are part of Jerusalem's obstinacy, misinterpreting the entry into the city as the commencement of Jesus' kingship rather than the way to his cross. Both their Christology and their eschatology are in error. (3) By placing the lament at the moment of Jesus' adoration by the crowds Luke shows that Jesus rejected any political interpretation of his entry into the city. (4) The sole purpose of the entry is for Jesus to take control of the temple (vv. 45–48). The profaners are driven out, and the temple becomes the place of Jesus' daily teaching (v. 47). The entry is not connected with the city per se at all; Jesus' proper place is the temple (cf. 2:49), he is its proper occupant, and when he leaves it at night he leaves the city also (21:37). It is then a matter of principle for Luke that the earliest Christian community remains loyal to the temple (Acts 2:46; 5:42). The destruction of the temple eventually occurs not because it is intrinsically wrong to worship in the temple, but because the profaners have reentered it and reexerted their control over it (Acts 7:51–53). The judgment that comes upon it is therefore a profane one and not a part of redemptive history (see Hans Conzelmann, *Theology of St. Luke* [New York: Harper & Row, Publishers, 1961], pp. 77–78, 164–65).

The "crying out of the stones" (cf. Hab. 2:11) in the verse immediately preceding our pericope is related to the acclamations of the multitudes; neither should be given unambiguous status as a believing confession. But Jesus acknowledges the reality of the cry for liberation and refuses to honor the suppression of the oppressed by the established authorities. Jesus' reply is full of pathos: "If you silence the oppressed, the stones would cry out." Such a cry for liberation presupposes humanity's fallenness; the cry itself does not presuppose the correct solution, the correct way out of bondage, and Jesus says that in v. 42. Yet part of the bondage is that inability to recognize the limits of human capability and to quit our calculating agendas to control God and his future. Jesus hears that cry for liberation and will have no part in its suppression, even though it is misguided. That it is misguided is cause for his grief, as is its silencing by those who fear open dialogue, for he knows the final result.

The house of God is not the place for the exercise of vested interests, even if they are carried on for the supposed convenience of the worshipers. It is the place where people acknowledge their dependence on God—and not vice versa. "No amount of sacrifices can substitute for surrender of the self" (Frederick W. Danker, *Jesus and the New Age according to St. Luke* [St. Louis: Clayton Publishing House, 1974], p. 199). The omission by Luke of the details of Jesus' action (rather violent in Mark 11:15–16) softens the impact of Jesus' wrath and places the weight on the Scripture cited by him (a combination of Isa. 56:7 and Jer. 7:11) as justification for his action. As Jesus' proper place, the temple is to be cleansed of profane vested interests.

Naturally persons representing such interests, instead of engaging in open dialogue and attempts at respectful persuasion, react according to their own agendas rather than God's. To destroy is so much easier, so much more final, than is the risk of repentance and growth. Luke's redaction of this pericope has consequences for its conclusion: the leaders who destroy the One whose rightful place is in God's house forfeit all lawful claim to preside there themselves.

But the good news of God's presence among his people through his prophet has its effect, as v. 48 wishes to say. God's word does not return to him void, and the faithful prophet, in spite of the dark night of struggle and the depths of inner pain, is always promised a hearing.

HOMILETICAL INTERPRETATION

The three passages suggested for this day contain some of the most moving and familiar words of all Scripture. The preacher needs to live with them and pray with them and wonder with them as well as study them. Occasionally the complaint has been made that the unity linking the passages suggested in this lectionary is difficult to discover. Sometimes that unity or common theme emerges as we give ourselves over to the readings in the life of feeling as well as in the life of the intellect. The Word may be made more available to the worshiping congregation if they have been encouraged in quiet reflection on the passages prior to the service or at least prior to the sermon. The preacher, as minister, needs to help enable that kind of devotional life which is not simply private prayer.

Such contemplation may suggest several important themes. One which presents itself comes most explicitly in the prelude to the Gospel pericope

> And when he drew near and saw the city *he wept* over it.
> (Luke 19:41 RSV, emphasis added)

If we continue the overall theme for the week as "The Story of the Death of Jesus," here we have a subtheme, "weeping."

A familiar story presents a child who has been sent to the neighborhood store to get a packet of yeast for her mother, who is waiting for the child's return in order to get on with the baking. The child does not appear when expected and her father is finally sent to hunt her up. He finds her coming down the sidewalk, delayed, but faithful to her errand.

"Where have you been?" he asks.

"I saw Maria. She had dropped her china doll on the sidewalk and smashed it all to pieces."

"And you stopped to help her pick up the pieces?"

"Oh, no. I stayed to help her cry."

So Jesus, weeping over Jerusalem, suggests the vocation of the church, his body: the church, weeping *with* the world, often before it knows its prized doll lies in pieces on that sidewalk, "where cross the crowded ways of life." Would not that hymn be sung with new strength in the shadow of this lesson? Consider especially the second stanza. Would not its last four words make an appropriate sermon theme *and* title?

> In haunts of wretchedness and need,
> On shadowed thresholds dark with fears,
> From paths where hide the lures of greed,
> We catch the vision of thy tears.
> (Frank Mason North)

Weeping with the world! This comes before the effort to pick up the pieces. Many churches in our time, urgent to put the pieces of the world back together and ease its "wretchedness and need," have skipped the "weeping," the "feeling." Then, before long, the motivation for putting things right is lost.

The person in the pulpit lacks the skill and expertise to prescribe all the appropriate remedies for world hunger and international conflict and disabling poverty and homelessness, but he or she has the responsibility so to sensitize the congregations of Christendom to the world's anguish that they will bring their expertise, as individual persons one by one and as the church as a whole, to bear on the problems. But the weeping, the feeling, the sharing of the pain comes first, and from that flows the energy for repair.

The preacher may also consider how this same truth applies in the personal as well as the public realm: broken marriages, tattered friendships, shattered reputations. Surely all this is appropriate spiritual discipline for the week of the death of Jesus; and it is absolutely necessary as prelude to participation in the resurrection. Is it related to the order of repentance and forgiveness?

Perhaps this theme will lead to another theme or concern: the nature of grief and its relation to spiritual and physical health. There is much material available to the preacher on this subject so far as personal bereavement is concerned. It may well be a part of the preaching during this pre-Easter week. Certainly many persons will be wondering if the comfort of the Easter story will possess them this year.

However, a reading of the First Lesson (Isa. 42:1–9) may broaden the grief to include sorrow for the death of the creation, the massive public deaths in waste of natural resources, abuse of the forests and the farmland, pollution of the sea and the air. The exegesis introduces us to the Hebrew word *mišpāṭ*. Congregations totally unfamiliar with Hebrew can be intrigued by the preacher's exposition of that word and its intention, along with *torah*, to express "the full scope of divine wisdom for all people and the world *in which they live*."

Consider vv. 5 and 9. The exegesis points out that the passage framed by these two verses "begins with reference to the God who has created the world and its inhabitants and concludes with reference to the 'new things' of the future which he has planned for them." Easter is a cosmic event, not only a personal one. Therefore, in preaching on "The Story of the Death of Jesus," the Holy Week story, one must not lose sight of its cosmic dimensions. This passage in the First Lesson directs us to remember that God is Lord of the *whole* creation.

Charles Birch, professor of biology at the University of Australia in Sydney, is helping stir the Christian world to this realization. "The immediate point of importance for us," he urged at a conference on "Faith, Science and the Future," "is that in the ecological view of nature, when the interests of people and elephants and kangaroos come into conflict, the nonhumans count for more than zero in the equation" (from a paper presented at a World Council of Churches conference at MIT, July 1979, and published in abridged form as "Nature, God and Humanity in Ecological Perspective" in *Christianity and Crisis,* 29 October 1979, p. 265; reprinted in *Faith and Science in an Unjust World* [Philadelphia: Fortress Press, 1980], p. 72).

Another theme is suggested by a reading of the lesson from Hebrews (11:39—12:3) alongside the Gospel lesson, which deals with Jesus' approach to Jerusalem and his visit to the temple, where he drove out the money changers. The verses in Hebrews remind us of the heroes of faith who were gypsies, on the move, on pilgrimage. Jesus also makes a pilgrimage, to Jerusalem, to the temple.

The expositor will find more here than one sermon can help set free. For example, the movement *before* the resurrection, *before* that cosmic event, is all *toward* Jerusalem. (Note the parallel spiritual movement of Jesus which the exegesis outlines from Heb. 12:2 and Phil. 2:5–11. That is another important aspect of this theme.) After that event, the movement is away from Jerusalem—up, out, and away to the whole inhabited world. This sweep says something about the nature of Christianity, about God's conclusive work in Christ. "Jesus is not just another link in the chain of heroic examples of faith." It also says something about the "ecological" concerns mentioned above ("Nature, God and Humanity," *Christianity and Crisis,* 29 October 1979, pp. 265–66):

> 'Twould ring the bells of Heaven
> The wildest peal for years,
> If parson lost his senses

And people came to theirs,
And he and they together
Knelt down with angry prayers
For slaughtered baby harp seals
And dancing dogs and bears
And harpooned great sperm whales
And little hunted hares.

The temple belongs to the old order. When God is able to change all that through Jesus' absolute obedience to love, shown forth in his weeping which carries him on to Calvary, persons begin to see that the faith is not centered in Jerusalem but out in the whole creation. The new is very dynamic, moving like the pilgrims in Hebrews, not an institution like the temple.

As preachers reflect on these verses, we may be moved to wonder about the church, the very congregation where this Holy Week preaching is being offered. Is the center of its life in the institution, the building, the organization, the rules, the doctrine?—or in the creation, including all the people within sight of its spire?

Someone else has suggested that the American railroads made a great mistake a few years ago: they thought they were in the railroad business instead of in the transportation business. As a consequence they were blind to other developing forms of transportation. If they had realized the true nature of their business, today they might own the airlines. So also with the church, this person claimed; when we believe we are in the "church business," a deadly narrowness sets in. The church as institution may be necessary to do the "people business" which is its real center. But when the institution takes over and seeks its own good, it needs upsetting.

We may want to ask our people to consider this truth as it bears on other institutions—the family, for example. Here as elsewhere the question of justice is crucial, but the expositor will do well to bear in mind the breadth of concept suggested by *mišpāṭ*. (See exegesis of Isa. 42:1–9.) Is the American family shaken today simply because of factors external to itself such as decline of an agrarian economy and the pervasive power of TV? Can the whole blame be placed there and personal responsibility avoided? Or is there more for Christians who are concerned for the values of family life to think about? Is the so-called Christian family getting a shaking up because there was some inherent injustice to women and children in it, even as promoted and endorsed by Christian persons and institutions? Did the adult male tend to *use* it for other ends than the good of its members or society at large? Note how politicians are urged by their managers to project a good family image if they want to be elected. Consider the pressure some American corporations are reputed to put on aspiring executives to *use* their wives for corporate advantage. (If that sounds like prostitution, so be it!) Does this differ morally from viewing children primarily as economic assets in an agricultural society?

These three passages spill over with words Christians have loved over the years and stories which give the expositor more material than can be helpfully used in a single sermon. However, there is one more to which the preacher's attention must be drawn: faith!

The exegesis reminds us that those rolling verses of Hebrews must be read in the context of other NT uses of the word "faith." It is not belief in a "body of doctrine." As we move with our people toward Good Friday and Easter Day through the preaching of these texts, it may be well to stress the fact that Christian faith is more a matter of trust than belief. It is sometimes helpful to suggest the difference between believing someone exists and believing *in* someone. We can weigh and measure all the objective sensory data, for example, and come to the conclusion that someone *does* actually exist. That may or may not be helpful depending upon the circumstances. It is quite another matter to be able to say on the basis of personal experience of someone else, "I believe *in* her or him." Indeed, note how much is added to that statement even as an illustration when you can insert the actual name of a real person, a beloved friend, a colleague, a son or daughter. So "faith" comes into substance and centers in the Person of Jesus in these passages. And toward his death we move.

Tuesday in Holy Week

Lutheran	Roman Catholic	Episcopal	Pres/UCC/Chr	Meth/COCU
Isa. 49:1–6	Isa. 49:1–6	Isa. 49:1–6	Isa. 42:1–9	Isa. 49:1–9a
1 Cor. 1:18–25		1 Cor. 1:18–31	1 Tim. 6:11–16	1 Cor. 1:18–31
John 12:20–36	John 13:21–33, 36–38	John 12:37–38, 42–50 or Mark 11:15–19	John 12:37–50	John 12:37–50

EXEGESIS

First Lesson: Isa. 49:1–9a. The second song of the servant of Yahweh, Isa. 49:1–6, along with a portion of the response to it (vv.

7–13), is the First Lesson for Tuesday in Holy Week. In the song itself we hear once again that the servant as a "light to the nations" is Yahweh's instrument to extend his salvation beyond the confines of Israel.

> [2]Yahweh called me from the womb,
> from the body of my mother he named my name.
> He made my mouth like a sharp sword,
> in the shadow of his hand he hid me;
> He made me a polished arrow;
> in his quiver he hid me away.
> [3]He said to me, "You are my servant [Israel];
> in you will I win glory."

As in other accounts of a prophetic calling found elsewhere in the Bible (cf. Jer. 1:5; Gal. 1:15), the servant is called before he was born; his prophetic activity did not begin on his own initiative. Yahweh chose him before he was active at all (while he was still hidden in Yahweh's quiver). He now is set aside as the one through whose mission Yahweh will be glorified. The brackets around "Israel" above are to indicate that the majority of exegetes consider it as a later insertion into the poem, inasmuch as it (1) metrically overloads the line and (2) is dissonant with v. 5, where Israel is the object of the servant's mission.

The servant's complaint (v. 4) and Yahweh's answer (v. 6) are reminiscent of the frustration of Jeremiah and Elijah over the apparent lack of response to their mission and God's renewal of the prophet's commission in even more specific terms. It brings the servant even more pointedly to the realization that the strength he has to carry on his mission comes from God alone (v. 5). Even though his mission to restore Israel is renewed (v. 6), that is now the lesser part of his mission. More importantly, the servant is to be a means of light and salvation to the nations. It is this far greater assignment which overcomes the prophet's frustration and anxiety, for it vindicates the prophet who is tempted to view the lack of response as his personal failure. The good news to him is that God will not be thwarted in his plan to bring light and salvation to all nations and in his desire to use his servant to achieve that goal.

Our pericope concludes with the first section of the response to the song, and again, as in the response to the first servant song, the speaker is Yahweh. It is precisely the object of universal contempt whom Yahweh uses to bring the nations to himself. It is God's agenda and no one else's. He has planned and he has chosen, he will answer and he will deliver in his own time. St. Paul has learned this lesson well, as the words following the Second Lesson for this day (1 Cor. 1:26—2:2) so clearly show. Vv. 8–9a are also reflected in Paul's discussion of the function of the Christian preacher in 2 Cor. 5:20—6:2, and v. 6b is used in the same way in Acts 13:47. In other words, Paul understands the mission of the servant to presage the mission of those who proclaim the gospel of Christ, and Luke's Paul finds in this second servant song the warrant and impulse for the church's mission to the Gentiles.

Second Lesson: 1 Cor. 1:18–25. In 1 Cor. 1:10–17 we have the portrait of a faction-ridden congregation whose divisions reached into the liturgical (cf. chap. 14) and sacramental life of the entire community (cf. 11:17–32 and our comments on the Second Lesson for Maundy Thursday). Vv. 12–16 suggest that the Corinthian Christians viewed baptism as a kind of magical rite in which the baptized person identified himself with the one who baptized him, sharing the latter's spirituality and "wisdom." Such "wisdom" was an achievement for the believer which enabled him to "know" the way of salvation and possess spiritual maturity. This attitude is noticeable if we read 2:14–15 as the claim of the Corinthians quoted by Paul, rather than his own position, a claim which is then answered by Paul in 3:14. The attainment of such "wisdom" became a mark of distinction in the church by which the Corinthians could test and compare one another (cf. 12:14–26; 2 Cor. 10:12); such spiritual maturity, they claimed, gave them a place far above the earthly world order (4:8).

Therefore preaching the cross of Jesus seemed to them to be folly, for the cross was the momentary triumph of the world and the forces of darkness, from whom they were now set free. It was Jesus' resurrection, mediated to them through their baptism, which freed them for life in the spirit. Such freedom is attainable *now,* without a future resurrection (15:12).

In response Paul insists that the word of the cross is the *power* of God (1:18)! It is God's power because that word destroys the wisdom of the wise (v. 19), for "the world did not know God through wisdom" (v. 21 RSV). Therefore God offers salvation through a word which could not be the product of worldly wisdom, which is in fact folly to the earthly world order.

What is worldly wisdom? It is seeking signs and proof—and offering them in return—to demonstrate that God is at work in us (v. 22). It is testing God by our criteria and attempting to "prove" his presence on the basis of our achievements. It is exhibiting our closeness with

God on the basis of our spiritual maturity, defined once again by us.

Therefore Christians proclaim Messiah Crucified: it is a word which destroys the criteria and standards of this world and its wisdom. It destroys all attempts to stand over against God and "prove" him on the basis of our own definitions. It does away with all our achievement, striving, and calculations. For the preaching of the cross is the message that the highest representative of possible human achievement, the Messiah, gave himself up to death, renouncing all striving before God, so that the life he would receive beyond it is nothing other than God's gift.

This is the strain of Paul's own theology which rings through the opening portion of this letter: Christ sent me to preach the gospel, and not with eloquent wisdom, lest the cross be emptied of its power (1:17). So we preach Messiah Crucified (1:23), so that no human being might boast in the presence of God (1:29). Therefore let no one boast of human beings; for all things are yours, whether Paul or Apollos or Cephas or the world or life or death or the present or the future—all are yours, for you are Christ's, and Christ is God's (3:21–23). What have you that you did not receive? If you received it, why do you boast as if it were not a gift? (4:7).

Gospel: John 12:20–36. This pericope relates perfectly on two fronts to the other lessons appointed for this day: (1) outreach to the Gentiles (Isa. 49), and (2) the meaning of Jesus' cross (1 Cor. 1). Chap. 12 in John's Gospel concludes Jesus' public ministry, following the Sanhedrin's decision to put him to death (11:53–57) and preceding Jesus' farewell discourses to his own (chaps. 13—17). Even though chap. 12 looks like a series of connected fragments which originally did not belong together (12:34–36 flows better after 8:29), it is composed with great artistry and gathers themes which are heard throughout the Gospel.

The pericope is held together by a series of implicit and explicit questions. Vv. 20–22 fulfill the fear expressed in v. 19 ("the world has gone after him!") and from the evangelist's point of view reflect the church's mission to the Gentiles. Yet the search of these Greeks is left unfulfilled in these verses! For the historical Jesus cannot be its fulfillment. The grain of wheat must first die. The Son of man must be lifted up (on the cross). Jesus' hour of glory, his death, is yet to come.

If the search for Jesus is to be of more than passing interest, if it is to be for discipleship, then at the outset it must be known what kind of discipleship it is to which Jesus draws (v. 32). When the two disciples announce the interest of the Greeks (v. 22), Jesus answers, "The hour has come for the Son of man to be glorified" (v. 23 RSV). The next question is, How is this to be done? The Greeks who have come to celebrate Passover know of the eschatological dimensions of the festival, of the coming of Messiah on Passover night to establish his triumphant rule. As gentile proselytes they know of the Son of man destined to come in glory to judge the world at the end of time. Is this the long-awaited moment of triumph and glory?

Vv. 24–26 provide the answer. Jesus' way to glory is the way of the cross. V. 24, reflecting the ancient notion of the actual death of the seed placed in the ground, explains Jesus' death as a prerequisite for the "bearing of much fruit." That is, Jesus' death is not an event which concerns just him alone, but *the* event of salvation history: it begins the gathering of his community, the drawing of all people to himself (v. 32), and as such is the hour of his glory. It also defines discipleship for those who wish to follow him (vv. 25–26).

Vv. 27–33 run parallel to vv. 20–26, depicting the decision of Jesus which makes possible the decision of the disciple who seeks after him. The synoptic agony in the garden (Mark 14:32ff. pars.) is here given its Johannine summation, complete with the strengthening from heaven (Luke 22:43). But John's emphasis is on Jesus' decision, not on the struggle of Jesus' soul. The decision to die, to reject the world's standards of calculation and achievement, striving and accomplishment, is a troubling one, but the one for which he has come and which will bear much fruit. It is not simply an example for others, but a decision whose result will open up the possibility for others to be free from the rule(r) of this world (v. 31). The heavenly voice in v. 28 recognizes that Jesus' decision to refuse the world's standards was not a momentary decision made once but one made throughout his ministry (cf. 17:4), a dying lived daily.

V. 34 poses the next explicit question: Isn't salvation in the future, in the glorious day of Messiah and the Son of man? Vv. 35–36 provide the answer: God and his revelation are bound neither to the future nor to our calculations about it. To believe, to have faith, is to be open to the present moment in which we are *now* called from darkness: "The light is with you for a little longer" (v. 35 RSV).

The disciple is not called to calculate about the future, to stand over against God and judge him by traditional criteria. The disciple is called to live the death of Jesus daily, by which all worldly standards and traditional criteria are judged. The disciple is called to be open to God's future, even in every present moment (v. 25), and thereby to believe: to see in Jesus' cross his hour of glory and the judgment of this world (v. 31). For that hour is the beginning of freedom from the world.

HOMILETICAL INTERPRETATION

"In the early summer of 1902 John Barrington Ashley of Coaltown, a small mining center in southern Illinois, was tried for the murder of Breckenridge Lansing, also of Coaltown. He was found guilty and sentenced to death." So begins Thornton Wilder's novel *The Eighth Day.*

Five days later John Ashley, under heavy guard, is on a night train, iron wheels rolling on and on relentlessly—on a narrow track—en route to the state prison. His destination was the *death house*. Then an astounding thing happened which his guards could not explain and the community could never understand but which none could deny.

John Ashley was rescued. He did not raise a finger. Six unarmed men somehow invaded the locked car, smashed the hanging lanterns, and without firing a shot or uttering a word overcame the guards and carried the prisoner off the train, the train bound for the death house. His rescuers snipped his handcuffs and the train rolled on. The rescuers receded into the darkness, and John Ashley breathed deeply the exhilarating air of freedom and new life, new birth, new joy.

We are attempting to deal with, interpret, appropriate the biblical passages suggested for Christians to read and hear expounded during Holy Week. The overall story, we have said, is "The Story of the Death of Jesus." But every Christian congregation where these lessons are read is open to signs and symbols of the resurrection. They know that these lessons, this story, "The Death of Jesus," are all leading up to Easter. That is the broader, the ultimate Christian context of their reading and of their exposition. Herman Waetjen once reminded us that we are like John Ashley in Thornton Wilder's story. We once were on a narrow track headed for the death house, but we also have been rescued. The cosmic Christ event, the resurrection, is already fact; the congregation where the reading takes place are the body of the resurrected Christ, participants in all the benefits thereof.

So we are like John Ashley; not only John Ashley the condemned but also John Ashley the rescued; not only en route to the death house but also delivered from that fate. We read and talk of death but we really are breathing deeply the exhilarating air of freedom and new life. So why then all this excessive, morbid concern with the *train of death?* Indeed, why go through Holy Week at all?

This question with all its ramifications and ways of presenting itself runs through the three lessons for this Tuesday in Holy Week. The exegete has brought it all to a helpful summary in the final sentences of his work opening up the text for us. But before we can fully understand it, we need to note another fact about John Ashley and us.

Although Ashley stood on the track a freed person, breathing the air of a new life, his situation was not unambiguous. This was not yet "Sabbath rest" to be spent in "endless praise." The rest of his life lay ahead of him. He could not return to Coaltown, to his past. A new future drew him into new responsibilities and obligations. He was free but he was bound! He had experienced objective power but he was confronted with subjective weakness! He had tasted eternal life but still faced temporality! He was in a double bind. And that double bind is the true situation of every Christian and of the church in all generations. So it is announced in the holy moment of the Eucharist: "Take and eat"—this is Christ, here present; but also and simultaneously, "You show forth Christ's death until he comes."

So the exegesis concludes, "To believe, to have faith, is to be open to the present moment in which we are *now* called from darkness. . . . The disciple is called to be open to God's future, even in every present moment . . ."

The tension which Thornton Wilder brought to life in the experience of John Ashley, freed from death but still bound to life, is a common underlying tension, explicit or implicit, in every Christian life, individual and corporate. The preacher working from these texts will discover many aspects of this fundamental tension.

The First Lesson (Isa. 49:1–9a) deals with the second song of the servant of Yahweh. The servant's complaint, "I have labored in vain," expresses a universal frustration and reminds us of the need to be linked in daily labor (walking down the track of freedom) to purposes which so transcend us that they are not judged by daily or yearly charts of success. A question Holy Week discipline and devotion presents to the believer: To what task are you committed which neither began with your birth nor will end with your death? Even as the servant was called (v. 1) from the womb, his task was designed by God before his birth and continues beyond his death. This week's preaching must help us place our lives in such divine perspective to provide meaning in the midst of apparent failure. To demand conclusions, completions, goals realized may be to court death rather than life. "Management by objective" may not be the last word of faith.

The Second Lesson (1 Cor. 1:18–25) deals with the manifestation of the tensions which this dilemma causes among the faithful. Paul has scolded the Corinthians for dividing up into cliques. (See vv. 11–12.) Our lesson can only be understood in light of the entire letter. Paul suggests that if you become purely spiritual, possessed by tongues (the sign of pure spirituality), you become self-centered in a narrow view of Christianity. It is as though John Ashley could live out the life of his freedom just standing on the tracks praising God. Even though he was "free" (or as Christians should we say, "because he was free"?), John Ashley had to walk into the future trustingly. (See the Isaiah lesson also for this reality!)

Paul is dealing with the false idea which was troubling the Corinthians that to be "in Christ" is a completion rather than a mode, an achievement rather than a "becoming." The preacher may want to track down the profound difference between the Greek view of maturity (an accomplishment like turning sixteen and getting your driver's license) and the biblical view (a "becoming"—a capacity to continue growth). John Ashley, standing on the tracks, turned away from death to life, still had a lot of "becoming" to do.

Somewhere Nels Ferré reports a bargain-basement counter full of shopworn crockery optimistically labeled "AS IS." Trying hard to make a sale, a salesclerk urges, "This vase, madam, is only *slightly* 'as is.'" To be "in Christ," to stand on the tracks of freedom, is not to be a new "as is" but is to become a "to be." It is to walk in the promise, not retire on an accomplishment!

The Gospel (John 12:20–36), as the exegesis explains, "gathers themes which are heard throughout the Gospel." All of these themes are again related to our overarching narrative for the week, "The Story of the Death of Jesus." Here there is explicit teaching in regard to Jesus' own death (vv. 32–34) as well as the well-known and existentially troubling word about the grain of wheat dying (v. 24) in order to live. All this material illuminates some of the earlier words in the Corinthian passage about "becoming" and about Christian maturity not being static but dynamic, not achievement but capacity for growth.

Holy Week preaching is often to the "faithful," that remnant who are always there if the church doors are open and without whom many a parish church long since would have disappeared. Is it not especially for such a congregation that the preacher may want to follow the leading of the exegesis in noting that this Gospel relates to the other lessons on two fronts—the outreach to the Gentiles and the meaning of the cross? Is it this loyal, faithful group (including the preacher) who most need to hear (even in the solemn devotions of Holy Week) that the church lives by mission and exists for those outside it?

Churches in transitional neighborhoods need to read and hear this part of "The Story of the Death of Jesus" carefully!

The Gospel and the synoptic parallels to which the exegesis calls our attention point up the element of decision in the road Jesus elected, that he was not the helpless pawn in power politics or destined by heredity or environment to "take up his cross" or "to be lifted up" (v. 32). Holy Week may be an appropriate time for the preacher to help us remember the profound difference between "a cross" and "a thorn in the flesh." There are many burdens which we cannot escape in life—physical and psychological handicaps, for example. Such burdens, however, are not necessarily "our cross," as some pious folk are wont to say. A "cross" is *voluntarily* assumed; free will is involved, a deliberate choice is made. "The Story of the Death of Jesus" must always keep this reality before us.

"To take up the cross daily" is the fashion of the becoming; it is the mode of the walking down the track in the time between our deliverance and the "return" of the Savior, between the "now" and the new Jerusalem. Our problem is in the waiting that must also be walking. All of which may bring us back to Thornton Wilder's liberated prisoner.

In the novel John Ashley's walking as a freed person into the future brings him one day many years later to South America far from the death house in Illinois. It was a day like many days for you and me. A woman with whom he had been affiliated in a rough kind of good works questions him about his dreams.

> "You look bad," she says, "You have not been sleeping. . . . You are having the dreams of universal nothingness. You think you will never be warm again. . . ."
>
> He turned from her and there was silence and he gazed out to the endless sea. She persisted. "You are forty-one or forty-two years old." She drew her finger across her face. "You have no wrinkles here—from care and thought. You have no wrinkles here—from laughter. Your understanding is like a little fetus—a poor little twisting and turning fetus—trying to be born."
>
> Then she handed him her crucifix. She pointed to the red glass beads that had been affixed to it to represent the drops of blood. She looked at him. "Red, red. Look at the red. Men, women, and children love you because of the blue of your eyes. But there is a better love than that. Blue is the color of faith. But red is love—every kind of love. Anybody can see that you have faith. . . . Faith is not enough. Maybe, if you are lucky, you will be born into love."

Wednesday in Holy Week

Lutheran	Roman Catholic	Episcopal	Pres/UCC/Chr	Meth/COCU
Isa. 50:4–9a	Isa. 50:4–9	Isa. 50:4–9a	Isa. 52:13—53:12	Isa. 50:4–9
Rom. 5:6–11		Heb. 9:11–15, 24–28	Rom. 5:6–11	Rom. 5:6–11
Matt. 26:14–25	Matt. 26:14–25	John 13:21–35 or Matt. 26:1–5, 14–25	Luke 22:1–16	John 13:21–38 or Matt. 26:1–5, 14–25

EXEGESIS

First Lesson: Isa. 50:4–9. See exegesis and homiletical interpretation from Sunday of the Passion.

Second Lesson: Rom. 5:6–11. Chap. 5 marks a new beginning in Romans, with the magnificent kerygma of the opening verse: "Therefore, since we are justified by faith, we have peace with God through our Lord Jesus Christ" (RSV). In 5:2–5 Paul stresses, as he does in his other letters, that justification does not release us from the struggles and sufferings of this world but gives us the sure hope that they will not overcome us. Such hope has its guarantee in God's love for us (5:5).

Vv. 6–8 identify that love of God with the death of Christ and portray the startling uniqueness of both. Vv. 9–11 summarize and restate the foregoing in terms of the reconciliation which now exists between God and his people. The section 5:12 through 8:39 deals with the ambiguity of a Christian existence which is on the one hand free from the tyranny of sin and death yet still subject to the effects of both (cf. esp. 8:22–25, 31–39).

Our pericope contains one of the most profound themes of Pauline theology, namely that the object of God's justifying grace is the sinner. The uniqueness of both God's love and the death of Christ is that they are for the *ungodly* (v. 6). V. 7a must then be taken with v. 6: it is not for the righteous that Christ died; they have no need for such an act, no need for God's justifying grace. We are reminded of Jesus' words in Mark 2:17 pars.: "Those who are well have no need of a physician, but those who are sick; I came not to call the righteous, but sinners" (RSV; cf. John 9:41).

V. 7b should now be seen in contrast to v. 8. Perhaps in the midst of the groaning of creation and the ambiguity of human existence, one person might in fact give his life for another good person. In fact, according to the world's standards such an act is warmly applauded. But the gospel breaks through the world's standards: God justifies not the good person but the sinner. Christ's death is for the ungodly (v. 8).

Without such justifying grace we are hopeless in this world, helpless against the tyranny of sin and death, party to the standards of this world and therefore estranged from God. But "at the right time" (= *kata kairon,* v. 6) Christ died for the ungodly. Paul takes great pains to specify "at the right time": "while we were helpless" (v. 6), "while we were sinners" (v. 8), "while we were enemies" (v. 10).

But now we are reconciled (vv. 10–11). The context defines the use of the word "reconcile" here. It does not refer to an inner experience either of the believer or of God, or to a sacrificial act which appeases an angry God, but to the objective event of the termination of estrangement. It is something which we have "received" (v. 11), accomplished without our efforts, while we were yet enemies. *Extra nos pro nobis* (outside of us and for us), it is the beginning of peace with God (5:1).

Therefore, our sufferings are not the result of God's wrath toward us but rather are manifestations of the realities of human existence, as we await in hope the final liberation from bondage and decay (cf. 8:21ff.). Yet in that arena we are no longer helpless but have access to God's grace and the gifts he gives us to endure (5:2–3). Reconciled by the death of his Son, Paul says, we are now saved by his life (v. 10). The life of the Crucified, by whose cross God has judged the standards of this decaying world, becomes our life and our escape from the tyranny of those standards.

Gospel: Matt. 26:14–25. It is beyond historical question that Judas's actions led to Jesus' arrest, for the church would hardly have invented the story that one of Jesus' own inner circle initiated the official procedure against him. Only Matthew mentions the precise amount of money—thirty pieces of silver—involved in Judas's transaction with the chief priests, and OT symbolism may be involved: (1) it is the price of a slave, Exod. 21:32; (2) it is also the wages of the shepherd of the flock in Zech. 11:12–13, a passage cited in Matt. 27:9–10.

As we mentioned above in our previous observations on the unique features of the Matthean passion narrative as a whole, Jesus is not carried along unknowingly by the rapid sequence of events but remains in control throughout. The brief section (26:17–19) on the preparation for the Passover, far briefer than Mark's account, demonstrates that point. In making preparations for the Passover meal, the disciples simply proclaim that the *kairos* of the Teacher has come, and doors are opened for them.

Matthew shows some discomfort about the precise Marcan dating of these events, omitting the identification of the day as that of the sacrifice of the Passover lamb (as in Mark 14:12 and Luke 22:7), which is carried out the day before Passover begins, and the reference to the man carrying a jar of water (as in Mark 14:13 and Luke 22:10), an action which might desecrate the observance. Nevertheless, Matthew retains the synoptic picture of the Last Supper as a Passover meal. Apart from this one section, however, nothing in Mark or Matthew would lead us to that conclusion. In John's Gospel the meal is an ordinary meal which takes place on the evening before Passover. Only Luke explicitly calls the supper a Passover meal (22:15), and all accounts lack mention of the prescribed ingredients of Exod. 12:1–13. At any rate, both problems, the chronology and the nature of the meal, are among the most puzzling in the NT. For details on the various attempted solutions, the reader is encouraged to see the commentaries on John by Rudolf Bultmann (*The Gospel of John* [Philadelphia: Westminster Press, 1971], p. 465) and Raymond E. Brown (*The Gospel according to John,* 2 vols., The Anchor Bible [Garden City, N.Y.: Doubleday & Co., 1966, 1970], pp. 555–56).

In Matt. 26:20–25 the traitor is identified in a dramatic way: "He who has dipped his hand in the dish with me, will betray me" (v. 23 RSV). The saying could simply mean that one of Jesus' closest companions is planning a treacherous act of betrayal. Mark and Luke seem to understand the saying in such light. But in Matthew the traitor is identified forthwith (v. 25). In the council meals at Qumran, according to the Rule of the Community (1QS) 6:1–8, the reaching out of the hands is to be done in hierarchical order (cf. also Josephus, *Jewish War,* II, 131). It has been suggested that Judas, by not waiting his turn and by dipping his hand into the dish at the same time as Jesus, has usurped the role of the leader and thereby has exposed himself as the one who is attempting to gain control.

V. 24 seems harsh, and it is. Stendahl refers to the interplay of determinism and free will as taught by the rabbis: what has to happen will happen, but that provides no excuse for the wrongdoer (M. Black and H. H. Rowley, eds., *Peake's Commentary on the Bible* [London: Thomas Nelson & Sons, 1963], p. 795, par. 693g). But v. 24 is related to vv. 23 and 25. This is the long-awaited *kairos* of the Son of man; *that* has been determined. And the one who has chosen his own agenda rather than God's must now live with what he has chosen; the one who attempts to usurp God's rule by living out of his own designs is subject to a future of insecurity and solitude, a fate not meant for those born as God's own. The end of Judas in Matt. 27:3–10 sadly confirms this.

Jesus' word is a strong word, and it functions less as a judgment pronounced on Judas than a direct word of warning to him. Jesus' answer to Judas's question "Is it I, Master?" (v. 25) throws the issue back to the questioner and asks him to deal with it. In Matthew Jesus does not expel Judas before distributing bread and wine as his body and his blood poured out for many for the forgiveness of sins. This may say something about Jesus' understanding of the supper and may recall his table fellowship with outcasts and sinners, his fellowship precisely with the unworthy! Is there a corrective there for our present-day eucharistic theology and practice?

HOMILETICAL INTERPRETATION

The first time I was invited to preach in Battell Chapel at Yale University I went with an excessively high level of anxiety. There were some of my former professors in the pews, and the entire scene made me very uneasy. At that time, as now, I was much indebted to the thought and writing of P. T. Forsyth, the British theologian, who had first helped me face up to the biblical concept of sin. In that first Battell sermon I quoted a familiar Forsyth phrase in this regard. "Sin," I said, and then quoting Forsyth, continued, " 'Sin, not public crime or private vice,' " then added in my own words and disastrously, "Sin, sin spelled with a capital C."

I do not recommend this kind of slip of the tongue, but I have remembered the theme of that sermon all these years. When we turn to the suggested lessons for Wednesday in Holy Week, we are dealing with "Sin." And it is spelled with a capital! Paul is not talking about "sins" with a small s, that is, wrongdoing which flows, in part, from Sin. But alas! I fear that is what most people think the preacher is talking about when the word "sin" comes from the pulpit. We need some other word to help our congregations understand that when the passages we are dealing with today lead us to discuss sin, we are wrestling with something far more pervasive and cosmic than theft or adultery or cruel gossip.

Herman Waetjen, who has stimulated my thinking about these passages greatly and to whom I am much indebted, urges us to substitute the word "plague" for Sin. He borrows the word from Camus and employs it in the sense of a universal human condition rather than individual acts. Much preaching in Christian churches remains trivial and moralistic and frequently destructive because of the manner with which the preacher deals with Sin and confuses it with its consequences, which may be sins. The use of the term "plague" can be helpful, and it will become real if the preacher remembers the stories of whole communities terrorized and brought low by ancient plagues and contemporary ones. A quick look at *Webster's New World Dictionary* under "Plague" will invigorate the preacher's language:

> 1. anything that afflicts or troubles; calamity; scourge. . . . 3. any contagious epidemic disease that is deadly; specifically, the bubonic plague. . . . v.t. 1. to afflict with a plague. 2. to vex, harass; trouble; torment.

Today's lessons, you will note, not only bring us back to Sunday's First Lesson but also offer us a stirring portion of "The Story of the Death of Jesus" as given in the Gospel at the beginning of the week. If we follow the narrative as the base and structure and theme of the sermon, we will turn first to the Gospel, Matt. 26:14–25. The exegesis dealt with Paul's abstract theology first, but the congregation will do better ordinarily with the story first. It is the story of the betrayal. They will be very quiet while it is read. Let us take our cue from that sign of interest. Let us fit Romans (the theoretical) into Matthew and use the theoretical to illumine the narrative rather than the other way around, where we articulate a theory or a doctrine and then illustrate it with a story.

Turning then to Matthew, we may find several details of the story which we may want to elaborate, all together or choosing only one. For example, the exegesis tells us that only Matthew mentions the precise amount of money, thirty pieces of silver. He also leads us to Zechariah 11. The reference is very helpful. It suggests why Matthew includes this detail about the thirty pieces of silver. This text needs to be linked to Matt. 27:5 where, after Jesus has been condemned and Judas has repented, he threw "down the pieces of silver in the temple." The "throwing down" may actually suggest a "down payment" more than a violent act. He put that money on deposit in the temple, for it was the termination of the old covenant: the price paid to end the power of the law. The end of the old covenant precedes the establishment of the new at the Last Supper, which is in our passage today. The payment to Judas comes *before* the supper. Now the One initiating the meal, Jesus Christ, will make the payment for the new covenant. To celebrate this meal with him means participating in this new community, freed of the plague. (This text might be more appropriate for Thursday night in many congregations, or in preparation for it.)

This narrative with the role of Judas emphasized then can provide a context for the crucial theory and doctrine introduced in the Second Lesson, Rom. 5:6–11. Here is the passage made famous by the Reformers for its continuing and central theological concern about sin and justification and reconciliation. The Judas story helps emphasize what the exegesis properly presses and Romans seeks to explain: the objective nature of the reconciliation effected by Christ's death. Reconciliation "does not refer to an inner experience either of the believer or of God, or to a sacrificial act which appeases an angry God, but to the objective event of the termination of estrangement."

The preacher may wish to introduce John Ashley again (see the homiletical interpretation for Tuesday). Ashley was not set free by his own efforts. He did not win it. It was a gift. There was an objective change in his total environment. That is, he was justified by faith through grace. When we swing along with some contemporary arrangement of "Amazing Grace," do we feel the "amazing" aspect of it? An achievement-oriented congregation can be baffled by all this language. It will need translation. The plague is over, the bad condition, the alienation, the separation, the death sentence; and we are John Ashleys, breathing freedom. That is good news. But it eludes us and baffles us and doubt persists.

Wilhelm and Marion Pauck write in their study of Paul Tillich that "it was from Kähler that Tillich gained the insight that man is justified by grace through faith, not only as a sinner but even as a doubter. The discovery of this idea brought him immense relief" (*Paul Tillich: His Life and Thought,* vol. 1 [New York: Harper & Row, Publishers, 1976], p. 19). There are many persons in our congregations who might find "immense relief" if the good news were made clear and real to them in relation to their struggle with doubt as well as with sins.

Another detail which the exegesis points up for us deals with "power." The preacher may wish to approach this theme with one or more of several emphases: power in personal relationships, power in vocation, power in marriage, power of a nation, power of international bodies. But the point upon which the drama of power in our story turns, and which can add great color and interest to the sermon, is the moment when Judas dips his hand in the dish at the same time as Jesus. (See exegesis.)

Another very heavy detail from these passages involves the matter of free will and *living with the consequences* of one's decision. Judas does not escape this. The preacher may wish to explore that theme in the light of the good news in Romans. Why is it that first we affirm of Christ in the Apostles' Creed that he "was crucified, dead, and buried," and then quickly and immediately add, "He descended into hell''? Can it be that the crucified Christ's first concern and first business always is with those who, like Judas, are in the consequences, the hell, of their own election?

If the pulpit is the channel of such grace, may we take care never to speak of it as ''Dr. So-and-So's pulpit.'' Bernard Manning once wisely said, ''The pulpit is no more the minister's than the communion table is.'' So may the preaching be a channel of ''amazing grace.''

Maundy Thursday

Lutheran	Roman Catholic	Episcopal	Pres/UCC/Chr	Meth/COCU
Exod. 12:1–14	Exod. 12:1–8, 11–14	Exod. 12:1–14a	Exod. 12:1–8, 11–14	Exod. 12:1–14
1 Cor. 11:17–32 or 1 Cor. 11:23–26	1 Cor. 11:23–26	1 Cor. 11:23–26 (27–32)	1 Cor. 11:23–32	1 Cor. 11:17–32
John 13:1–17, 34	John 13:1–15	John 13:1–15 or Luke 22:14–30	John 13:1–15	John 13:1–17, 34

EXEGESIS

First Lesson: Exod. 12:1–14. Historically the Passover, which by the NT period had become the major Jewish festival, had its beginnings within a nomadic culture. It was not bound to one sacred location, and it was carried out not by priests but by the elders of the clan. The blood sprinkled on the entrance to the tents had an apotropaic function, that is, to ward off evil, to protect people and their herds from the demons of the wilderness (cf. ''the destroyer,'' vv. 13 and 23). In an important study in 1943, L. Rost suggested that the danger from which the blood ritual offered protection was greatest when the nomads transferred their herds each spring from the desert to the cultivable land for summer pasture, a time when the newborn lambs and kids faced many threats to their lives along the way. Other scholars have suggested that the nomadic blood ritual became connected to the Canaanite new year's *(mazzot)* festival in the spring, when the first yield of the barley harvest was prepared and eaten unleavened. Eventually the two were combined, with the former dominating to give the festival the name *pesach,* and later Passover. How did Israel incorporate *pesach-mazzot,* based on the rhythm of nature and the cycle of the seasons, into its faith and life so that it became a "Passover for Yahweh" (vv. 11, 14, 27)?

First of all, by joining it to the Exodus the dangers of Israel's own journey from Egypt to Canaan were recalled (v. 14), and the situation of hurried flight (v. 11) was maintained in the rite. Secondly, the name of the festival was declared Passover (*psḥ* vv. 13, 23, 27—although the actual etymology of the word *pesach* is still not known). Israel was afforded protection by Yahweh from the demons of the wilderness, and the "destroyer" (v. 23) became subject to him (v. 23). Thirdly, by subordinating the destroyer to Yahweh, who led them out of Egypt, the annually recurring threat of the demons of nature is understood as removed in the once-and-for-all act of the God who still remains with his people, and whose people remember his deed in history by the celebration of it as a memorial (v. 14). Finally, by setting the memorial on a fixed date (vv. 3ff.), the fifteenth day of the first month of the year (Nisan), rather than using some annual event in the realm of nature having to do with the care of the flocks or the crops, the immediate attachment of the festival to a season of nature was diminished. The chief place on the calendar was given to Passover. (The later Jewish New Year's festival, *rosh ha-shanah,* was not known in OT times.) Passover was then bound to the event of the Exodus, and Exodus 12 must be read with Exodus 13.

Exod. 12:1–13 describes the preparation to take place during the period immediately preceding the fifteenth day of Nisan, the first Passover. Vv. 14–20 are concerned with the particulars of the cultic celebration of Passover and *mazzot* as a memorial of Yahweh's deliverance of his people from Egypt (v. 17). Like the ancient *pesach* the celebration takes place in the family circle. Only the later Deuteronomic code (Deut. 16:2, 5–7) and Josiah's reform (2 Kings 23:21ff.) shifted it to the temple. Unlike the ancient *pesach,* it is now a "memorial" *(zikkaron);* that is, it is no longer apotropaic—a protection against evil forces, a charm to be repeated to guarantee security—but a remembrance of the one act by which Yahweh has delivered his people from evil once and for all. For the Hebrew a "memorial" does not produce simply mental recall but a reexperiencing of the original event; therefore the fixed date, the unleavened bread and bitter herbs, the roasted lamb, the eating with haste. To reexperience Passover is to reexperience identity with the people called into being and delivered by God.

Christian proclamation of this text on Maundy Thursday will best avoid all attempts to prove the external connection between Passover and the last meal Jesus shared with his disciples, especially since our Gospel for this day is from the Fourth Gospel, which represents the meal in a very different way. The depiction of Jesus himself as the Passover Lamb by both John (1:29) and Paul (1 Cor. 5:7) will move us to seek a deeper, internal connection, so that God's good news can be heard from the text, rather than the probabilities of historical data. In order to do this we must, however, allow ourselves to be informed by historical research, to detect the alternatives residing in the text which enable the task of kerygma.

As in the ancient nomadic *pesach,* God still calls his people together in families, providing the means for their survival in the face of the hostile forces of this world. The individual has a relationship with God and avails himself of its benefits only by virtue of his identity as a member of the group. The established religious order and its permanent shrines are secondary, for neither God nor the nomads are bound to any "abiding city" in this world. Their eating hastily, prepared for flight, indicates their openness to God's future and his appointed time, their existence not determined by the condition of this world and its forces.

The kerygma of Passover is that the ritual itself, unlike that of the ancient *pesach,* is not a charm, a device by which *we* guarantee our safety and the favor of God over against the demons. In 1 Cor. 10:1ff. St. Paul has captured the profundity of Passover, Exodus, and Lord's Supper: the ritual ceremony itself is no guarantee of this-wordly security, even if it signals the presence of God. The ritual is not a charm but a memorial, a remembrance, by which the participants reexperience their identity with the God who called them into being and delivered them, and by whose action they know who they are.

Our identity is determined not by the forces of nature and the seasons of the year (and as we approach Easter, neither should our preaching be!) but by the God who acts in history. Passover celebrates his action in the Exodus, which determines our present and future existence. The Lord's Supper celebrates his action in Jesus' death and resurrection, which determines our present and future existence. Both Passover and the supper are "memorials," calling us to remember the God who has acted to give us our identity, to make us his own and be called by his name.

Looking back, we can also look forward—Jews and Christians—to the God of promise who controls both past and future, and who promises never to forsake his people. And if we all, Jews and Christians, look forward to his future and allow him to determine the form that future might take, can there not be among Jews and Christians "a common sharing of God's joy which links the *seder* and the eucharist into common praise?" (Brevard Childs, *The Book of Exodus* [Philadelphia: Westminster Press, 1974], p. 214).

Second Lesson: 1 Cor. 11:17–32. If we read the Corinthian letters as *letters,* occasioned by specific questions the Corinthians put to Paul (1 Cor. 7:1), we shall be impressed by Paul's firm pastoral approach in attempting to speak from a distance (Ephesus; see 16:8) to a faction-ridden community which is now beginning to call his authority over them in question (chap. 9). Because he loves them as their spiritual father (4:15 asserts that he founded the church in Corinth; cf. Acts 18), he must speak the firm word so as not to alienate but rather to restore. For he is aware of the splinter groups in the congregation (1:11; 11:18) and their harmful effects on the church, especially in the worship assemblies (11:17).

The gravity of the problem is that the very validity of the Corinthians' Eucharist as the Lord's Supper is at stake: "When you meet together, it is not the Lord's supper that you eat. For in eating, one goes ahead with his own meal, and one is hungry and another is drunk" (11:20–21 RSV). In other words, individualism at the expense of community has no place at the Lord's Supper. How did such individualism threaten the community's Eucharist at Corinth?

At Corinth the eucharistic celebration included a regular meal (cf. v. 25) in which the members of the congregation ate together, each contributing to it according to his own means. This connection between communal meal and sacrament is reflected in the accounts of the Last Supper in the synoptic Gospels (cf. Mark 14:22). The sacramental act itself was, of course, the high point of the celebration, taking place most likely at the end, as Didache 10:1 puts it, "after you are satisfied with food." In Corinth the problem centered not so much on the actual sacramental act as on the Corinthians' behavior and the attitudes behind such behavior during the common meal. The divisions in the congregation (1:11) are now mentioned in this context (11:18), and when 11:21 is read with 11:33, it seems that the system of cliques has carried over into the eucharistic celebrations. At the common meal factions evolved as self-interest prevailed: one took one's own meal in the company of one's own peers, friends, relatives, societal or ideological group. We can readily understand the human tendency to socialize with one's own, with those of like mind, of like color, of like social status. The wealthier members of the congregation brought their well-supplied baskets to the communal gatherings and feasted with their own, while the less well-off, workers and slaves who could not leave their work so easily and who arrived late, were left with nothing.

For Paul, communal meal and Eucharist at Corinth cannot be separated. The whole concept of the church is at stake: "Do you despise the church of God and humiliate those who have nothing?"

(v. 22). Factions at the expense of the community invalidate the celebration as the Lord's Supper because it is the *Lord's* church which is being fractured, and therefore despised. The Lord, whose presence is invoked, does not preside over festivities which allow members of his body to be humiliated. His body, the church, belongs to him, and not to those who would recreate it in their own image. Therefore Paul's words in v. 29: "For anyone who eats and drinks without discerning the body eats and drinks judgment on himself." It is a profound statement and has first of all to do with understanding what the church is. But there is also another dimension to the statement: if a person cannot see in the church the body of Christ, then he will not see it in the bread and wine either. Then the body and blood of the Lord are profaned (v. 27), such a participant's action is not under Jesus' sponsorship, and he is judged (v. 29). At Corinth the congregation as a whole has invited such judgment on itself (vv. 30–32): some have grown weak, then ill, then have died—because they have not cared for each other; they have not seen in each other members of the body of Christ. Such judgment is not to be seen as God's final condemnation, and if it is from the Lord, it comes as gracious discipline so that the whole body will be preserved from the world and its judgment.

It is in the midst of this discussion that Paul inserts the words of institution as "tradition" which he himself has received. That he has received it "from the Lord" is not reference to a special revelation to him alone from the exalted Jesus but a tradition mediated from the time of the earthly Jesus through the church, and as such it is a word "from the Lord" (cf. 1 Thess. 2:13). The words of institution here cited may be the earliest version found in the NT and in fact predate Paul, representing formulated eucharistic practice as early as the 30s A.D. (For a detailed comparison of this version with the synoptic texts, see Gunther Bornkamm, "Lord's Supper and Church in Paul," in *Early Christian Experience* [New York: Harper & Row, Publishers, 1969], pp. 121–60.)

The traditional words of institution in vv. 23–25 are followed by Paul's own explanatory statement in v. 26. The way they are juxtaposed here suggests that Paul is not speaking to any possible heretical understanding, use, or nonuse of the sacramental rite itself. Rather, his intention is to relate the rite as a whole to the actual life of the congregation. His explanatory sentence in v. 26 contains two ingredients in the eucharistic formula which speak to this concern: fixed date and remembrance.

It is striking that while there is nothing in 1 Corinthians 11 which indicates Paul's understanding of the Last Supper as a Passover meal, these two ingredients, fixed date and remembrance, recall vividly two basic features of Exodus 12 (see discussion of the First Lesson). The fixed date, "on the night in which he was betrayed," anchors the Lord's Supper to a given event in history, namely the Lord's death, and not to a repeatable cycle of mythical events influenced by cultic reenactment. It is the Lord's death which is also the object of remembrance at the Eucharist. As a remembrance the Lord's Supper is not apotropaic, that is, a charm to ward off evil and guarantee security ("some have died," v. 30; cf. 10:1ff.). Like Passover, the Lord's Supper is a remembrance of the act in history by which God has delivered his people and given them their identity. Paul has here understood "remembrance" in the profoundest Hebrew sense of the word *zakar,* not as simple mental recall but as a reexperiencing, an appropriation of the event of the Lord's death for one's own existence. In the Lord's Supper Christians are called to reexperience identity with the people called into being and delivered by God in the death of Jesus. So Paul can write elsewhere (Gal. 2:20), "I have been crucified with Christ; it is no longer I who live, but Christ who lives in me; and the life I now live in the flesh I live by faith in the Son of God, who loved me and gave himself for me."

Eucharist so defined will restore to the communal meal and to all other congregational relationships the perspective of a community called to live the life of the Crucified. The cross of Jesus is the moment Messiah gave up all claims for himself, and the life he received beyond it is nothing other than God's gift. Living the life of the Crucified, then, means giving up all claims for rank and privilege before God, so that we see all that we have—our lives, our congregations, our abilities, our families and friends—as God's gift to us. Exploitation will be turned into service, and striving for ourselves into ministry for others.

Gospel: John 13:1–17, 34. John does include a "last supper" which Jesus shares with his disciples, but in place of the eucharistic words over the bread and wine there is a foot washing and its interpretation, the traditional Gospel for Maundy Thursday. The ancient inclusion of v. 34 in the lesson has undoubtedly contributed the name of this day in Holy Week. For the word "Maundy" is derived from the Latin word used in the Vulgate in v. 34, *Mandatum (novum),* the (new) commandment Jesus gave to his disciples that they should love one another as he has loved them.

After a remarkable, lengthy introduction (13:1–3), the narrative breaks into two parts: (1) the foot washing (vv. 4–11), with an exchange between Peter and Jesus, and (2) the interpretation of the foot washing (vv. 12–20), ending with a cluster of sayings including reference to the betrayer. The richly expansive introduction serves as a preface not merely to the foot washing but also to the whole of chaps. 13—17; Jesus' hour has come, and chaps. 13—17 are his farewell discourses. In chap. 18 John's passion narrative begins.

Jesus' hour has come. Already the decision to do away with him had been made (11:53, 57). Preparation for his burial was already under way (12:7). What remains is his farewell to his own, which means that everything that Jesus says and does in chaps. 13—17 is said and done in the light of his cross. His cross is the hour of his glory (13:31; 17:1), a theme heard throughout the Fourth Gospel (3:14; 11:4 is to be read in light of 11:53; 12:23–24, 27–28). It is the reason for which he has come (12:27).

To their astonishment, Jesus begins to wash his disciples' feet, the master performing the duty of a slave. The meticulous detail of his actions recorded in vv. 4–5 serve to heighten the contradiction inherent in this scene. Peter's reaction is quite inevitable, very human, and therefore readily understandable: "Lord, are *you* going to wash *my* feet?" Jesus replies: "You may not realize now what I am doing, but afterward you will understand." Again Peter demurs: "You shall never wash *my* feet!" To which Jesus responds: "If I do not wash you, you have no part in me."

This interchange is not easy to understand. It should not be approached in cavalier fashion, and attempts at psychologizing both participants are not productive. What is clear, however, is that there is something far more important at stake than the disciples' clean feet. The "afterward" *(meta tauta)* of v. 7 constitutes the focal point from which this scene will at last be understood—for Peter, for the disciples, for us. That focal point is nothing other than Jesus' imminent "hour," namely his death on the cross.

As the cross is scandalous to some (1 Cor. 1:23), this scene is scandalous to Peter, and his reaction is "natural," profoundly human. That the master is a slave is a breach in the system, a violation of the world's standards. That Jesus' cross is the event by which the world is redeemed is an absurdity, foolishness to the natural human mind. As long as God stays in his heaven, all can be right with the world. But when he becomes one of us, our categories of sacred and profane are called in question. The cross of Jesus does just that: our standards for that which is triumphant, respectable, and worthy are called in question. So Bultmann: "Peter's words . . . express . . . the basic way men think, the refusal to see the act of salvation in what is lowly, or God in the form of a slave" *(Gospel of John,* p. 468).

But Peter's reaction is profoundly human also for another reason. Peter has difficulty in *receiving* what is a gift, for the recipient is no longer in control of the transaction. Therefore Jesus' words, "If I do not wash you, you have no part in me," mean that Peter's relationship with Jesus (and thus with God) is a gift to Peter, not of his own doing. The good news seems too good to be true: God has channeled his favor to us through his Son, as a gift. But haven't we accomplished something to earn God's favor and to secure our relationship with him? Peter's remark in v. 9 is such an attempt to guarantee it, and Jesus' reply (v. 10) is that he does not need to. It is guaranteed, by God's action alone.

The meaning of v. 10 is disputed on textual as well as exegetical grounds. The phrase "except for his feet" is lacking in Codex Sinaiticus, Origen and Tertullian, and some Vulgate witnesses. It is probably not original but was appended by an ancient scribe who, understanding the phrase "he who was bathed" to refer to the baptized, added the exception to show that Jesus was not excluding ceremonial foot washing. Without the addition, the verse is directed against all attempts to use any ritual as a charm, or as a guarantee of salvation. With the addition, the verse might seem to make foot washing an exception to the general rule. But v. 11 reminds us that even the foot-washing ceremony enacted by Jesus himself in this scene did not guarantee the purity of Judas. V. 10, then, should be read in the light of 15:3: "Already you are clean, because of the word I have spoken to you." That is a word *received*, through believing. Vv. 12–20 interpret the foot washing in a slightly different way: in 4–11 it was an action symbolic of what Jesus has done for his disciples, and God through him; in 12–20 the foot washing becomes the basis for *imitatio Christi* among his followers. Once again, however, Jesus' discourse strikes far deeper than ceremonial piety or ritualistic *imitatio*. Jesus' call to do as he has done is a word which challenges human standards and rules in the light of his cross.

It is a new commandment we hear on Maundy Thursday: "that you love one another as I have loved you." That word binds us in community with each other, the fellowship of those who receive. The meal we share joins us together as recipients and makes us servants of one another, for our cleansing is not by ourselves but by the word Jesus speaks: "as I have loved you."

HOMILETICAL INTERPRETATION

Somewhere Willa Cather suggests that we sense the miracles of the church not so much in faces or voices or sudden healing as in our perceptions' being sharpened. Then we are enabled to be aware of what has really been there all the time.

If preachers will read through the three passages suggested for Maundy Thursday in this lectionary and then read through the exegesis for the day, they will surely feel their perceptions deepening with power and broadening with gentleness. These familiar passages begin to burst with unsuspected energy and unity as they interact with each other and are read and heard in the larger context of this week's overarching theme, "The Story of the Death of Jesus." It is my desire that the homiletical interpretation especially for this very special day (and night!) in the Christian year will not hinder that perception but be in league with it. Let us look at some of the material.

Even here it is well to begin, as proposed at the outset of the week, with the narrative part of the material and regard it as basic. It may help the homiletician to think of the sermon as a bouquet being created to the glory of God and for the love of mankind. The narrative might be considered the rich, deep, luxuriant green foliage which forms the base and background and "holding-up" material for the bouquet. Then from the other passages and human experience color and life are added like the variety of blossoms in a spring arrangement. One might begin and end at the very end of the Gospel with that single thirty-fourth verse: "A new commandment I give to you, that you love one another; even as I have loved you, that you also love one another." Many congregations need help to remember that this is the basis for the name of the day, Maundy Thursday, as explained in the exegesis; and then the story in the Gospel or the implicit narrative in the Second Lesson may be spread upon or around that single crucial verse.

Preaching on this day, of all days, should center on the Eucharist; and if one does not intend actually to observe the foot-washing ceremony, one may want at least to have bowl, pitcher, and towel in evidence. Then we will see and feel more quickly our identity with Peter, resisting the gift, resisting the story, resisting the action.

The exegesis suggests two reasons for the resistance, and these could be the basis of a two-point sermon. Both of Peter's reasons bear contemporary interpretation: For one thing, Christ upsets the presuppositions. The master becomes the slave. Here is the divine reversal, the breach in the "system," the holy absurdity: weakness is power and the powerful are brought low. The preacher's temptation is to use this as a threat, scolding the congregation, especially when the pulpit stands in the midst of the powerful, the dominant people of an American town, or of Western culture, or before institutional "greats"—physicians or brokers or college presidents or labor leaders. Always better not to scold. To preach is not to scold or advise but to proclaim. Here, then, proclaim this foot washing as the "ultimate beauty" and not the "ultimate rebuke" (they may be kin!), and allow its drawing power to set us free.

Jonathan Edwards, who believed that beauty was the principal clue to the nature of reality, also declared that God governs not by brute force "but by the attractive power, that is, the beauty of the apparent good." Is it not the beauty in Jesus' action which condemns us and draws us and saves us?—not scolding by preachers who have not stopped long enough before that beauty. It is significant to note that Edwards, who is remembered in the popular mind for his Enfield sermon, "Sinners in the Hands of an Angry God," chose 1 Corinthians 13, the chapter on love, as his text when he preached the revival in his own home church. It was Edwards who, preaching for a religious experience, for regeneration, always maintained that the first effect of regeneration was to give the "heart a relish for the loveliness of the supreme excellency." We have here a moving part of the total drama of the "supreme excellence." Peter resisted because what Jesus did upset the system.

In the second place Peter also resisted, as the exegesis suggests, because it required him to receive. We are told that it is "better to give than to receive." The verse has been repeated so often, so thoughtlessly, and so one-sidedly, that it has become dangerously misleading. Many years of parish ministry lead me to believe that most earnest Christian people find it much easier to give than to receive. We want to be "up and doing," especially for people we love, winning points, achieving appreciation (love), good works. That's really easy. How hard to be the recipient of another person's gift to us! So with Peter. The preacher may wish to explore this claim.

Perhaps in our time the church needs as much to receive as to give, not only from God but from other human beings on this planet. Is there any "missionary" effort which has any promise to reach Marxism or Buddhism or the whole Muslim world except one which is prepared to receive from them? We are all ready to give to them, our wisdom, our values, our Jesus. But until we can be open to receive, can they accept? Our earlier work this week on justification by faith bears on this point. Good works are endless giving. Faith is endless receiving. In the solemnity of Maundy Thursday, the beauty of Christ's own portrayal of this truth may move us. The sermon itself can only be an instrument for it. At this moment every preacher will surely hear James Denney: "No man can give at once the impression that he himself is clever and that Jesus is mighty to save."

The Second Lesson (1 Cor. 11:17–32) is a subtheme of the tremendous "caring" drama in the Gospel. It suggests a sermon which will be warmly pastoral in tone and purpose. Paul is addressing a congregation split and spiritually impoverished. What a searing indictment: "When you come together it is not for the better but for the worse" (v. 17 RSV). He goes on to lament in particular the manner in which they celebrate the Lord's Supper. There may be wide speculation about what the practice was in the early church, but the violation of their meeting together was clear. They "despised" the church of God and "humiliated" those who had nothing (v. 22).

What about other church suppers? They are an institution in American Protestantism: potluck, picnic basket, or catered by a French restaurateur! But what happens to *people* at them? Remember the scene in the musical *Oklahoma* where the box lunches are auctioned off with the young men bidding up the one prepared by the popular and attractive young woman while the lunch brought by the awkward one is neglected? What pain groups inflict on their own members! How destructive that country custom must often have been! And church suppers today—chairs turned up and reserved for special friends are chairs turned up rejecting friendship of those present. How many kinds of chairs are "turned up" in the common life of an American parish? I wonder if something like this was not happening in Corinth, humiliating "those who have nothing"!

Paul is talking about the quality of parish life. That quality may be demonstrated more at the church supper than at the Lord's Supper. Elsewhere I have written at length about the poignant need in American society for communities of acceptance, where loneliness is ended in a genuine relationship with other human beings (Browne Barr, *The Well Church Book* [New York: Seabury Press, 1976]). That book seeks to lay out many practical things that can be done to nourish such community in the local church. One of them is to preach concretely and pastorally from time to time on texts like any one of the three suggested for this day. Another is to take seriously the theological reality which Karl Barth underscores when he writes, "Take good note, that a parson who does not believe that in this congregation of his, including those men and women, old wives and children, Christ's own congregation exists, does not believe at all in the existence of the church. *Credo ecclesiam* means that I believe that here, at this place, in the visible assembly, the work of the Holy Spirit takes place" (*Dogmatics in Outline,* trans. G. T. Thomson [London: SCM Press, 1949], p. 145).

The First Lesson may be the most important one of all for this day. At first reading all three of these selections may amaze the preacher. But their relationship to one another and to the story of the week emerges. The Corinthians lesson includes the oldest account of the Lord's Supper in the entire Bible, and the First Lesson describes the preparation for the Passover. Sometime during this week the Exodus theme needs serious treatment, to prepare a congregation to incorporate the experience of which they will sing on Easter Day:

> Come, ye faithful, raise the strain of triumphant gladness;
> God hath brought his Israel into joy from sadness;
> Loosed from Pharaoh's bitter yoke Jacob's sons and daughters;
> Led them with unmoistened foot through the Red Sea waters.
> (Attributed to John of Damascus, c. 696–c. 754)

The preacher may do well to bring the Exodus passage and the Corinthians passage to join the Gospel narrative in emphasizing the historicity of the crucial Christian "remembrance." The Exodus and the Resurrection were both alike the action of God in history. When Christians get too abstract, "too spiritual," it is well to ask for evidence of the absolute continuity between the Jesus of history and the Christ of faith—in action. When we meet on Maundy Thursday and submit to the discipline of the Word and prepare "to receive," we are anchored to an event, a historical reality, not a philosophical concept. Such an experience may prepare us to participate in Resurrection Day.

Good Friday

Lutheran	Roman Catholic	Episcopal	Pres/UCC/Chr	Meth/COCU
Isa. 52:13—53:12 or Hos. 6:1–6	Isa. 52:13—53:12	Isa. 52:13—53:12 or Gen. 22:1–18 or Wisd. 2:1, 12–24	Isa. 52:13—53:12	Isa. 52:13—53:12
Heb. 4:14–16; 5:7–9	Heb. 4:14–16; 5:7–9	Heb. 10:1–25	Heb. 4:14–16; 5:7–9	Heb. 4:14–16; 5:7–9 or Heb. 10:1–25
John 18:1—19:42 or John 19:17–30	John 18:1—19:42	John (18:1–40) 19:1–37	John 19:17–30	John 18:1—19:42 or John 19:17–30

EXEGESIS

First Lesson: Isa. 52:13—53:12. In Acts 8:26ff. the evangelist Philip is asked by an Ethiopian official reading this fourth servant song to explain who it is of whom the prophet is speaking. Who is the servant who is led like a sheep to the slaughter, who like a lamb before his shearers opens not his mouth? As long as the church reads this pericope on Good Friday there will be no question in any worshiper's mind about the identification of the servant. For like Philip, the church throughout the ages has seen in this text the perfect opportunity to proclaim "the good news about Jesus" (Acts 8:35).

The necessity to identify the servant with only one figure in history is, however, hardly supported either by the songs themselves or, as we have seen in our previous comments above, by the NT writers. The movement between individual(s) and group goes back to the earliest interpretation of the songs, in fact to the text of the songs themselves. The figure of the servant is understood by its ancient interpreters as a "tensive" symbol, that is, a symbol whose meaning is neither exhausted nor adequately expressed by any one referent. The servant is the instrument of God, who, precisely because he is without power and recognition, is the one through whom *God's* saving power is recognized. Yes, the servant is Israel, the slave of nations, whose testimony to Yahweh is set as an inextinguishable beacon to provide rescue to the nations bound in darkness. Yes, the servant is the quiet proclaimer of God's good news, the powerless minister whose message is powerful only because God has made it so. Yes, the servant is Jesus the Crucified, whose willingness to lay down all claims to power and achievement before God enables him to receive his future as God's gift. Yes, the servant is the innocent sufferer(s) of today, by whom the world and its standards are judged and through whom the surprise of God's redemptive rule can be seen.

The surprise of the nations, a theme heard in the response to the second servant song, is heard most vividly in the fourth song, the First Lesson for Good Friday, Isa. 52:13—53:12. At the outset the servant's vindication is promised (v. 13), which presupposes his humiliation among the peoples, who are then astonished at his vindication (v. 14). The servant's humiliation to the point of his death is described in 53:1–9. How easy it was for us to see his plight as God's doing (v. 4b) rather than as participation in our own brokenness (vv. 4a, 5–6). In fact, it is precisely in his participation in humanity's brokenness that God's vindication of the servant is sealed (vv. 10–12; of the translations NEB is preferable):

> 10Yet Yahweh took pleasure in his humiliated one and healed the one who made his life an offering for sin.
> He will see his children's children and enjoy long life, and in his hand Yahweh's cause shall prosper.

The surprise of the nations at the servant's humiliation means that his suffering is not a calculated action on his part, nor does he have a psychotic mentality which simply enjoys flagellation. They do not expect what they see. He is one of them, with little distinction from them and with no apparent reason for his plight (v. 2). How easy, then, to conclude that he is under God's judgment—until we contemplate what his solidarity with us really means! Are we under such judgment also? After all we've done for God! How astonishing, then, to see that it is precisely the humiliated one who is the object of God's vindication! Why him and not us? The very raising of that question shows us why his vindication was for our sake.

The life (Heb. *nephesh*) of the servant, lived as an "offering for sin," causes that question to be raised. Again and again the song emphasizes the vicarious nature of the servant's offering: borne our griefs, carried our sorrows, wounded for our transgressions, bruised for our iniquities, his chastisement made us whole, with his stripes we are healed, our iniquity is laid on him. Here exegesis must not overstep its bounds and become embroiled in debating the nature of the sacrifice (Heb. *asham* = "guilt offering"), for only here in the entire OT is it stated that a person's life can be a guilt offering. Perhaps all we should say is that the connection between the vicariousness of the servant's giving up of himself and the astonishment of the people guarantees that the servant's life will now assume a central role in the relationship between God and his people. His action insures the knowledge that our achievement before God is not what makes us righteous. The knowledge (the owning) of servanthood, that is, the quitting of all calculation and achievement before God, will lead many—us—to be accounted righteous (v. 11). Not by ourselves, but by God the Vindicator.

The structure of the song is that of a sequence: a speech by Yahweh (52:13–15); a chorus (53:1–10); a final speech by Yahweh (53:11–12). The striking feature is that the speeches of Yahweh proclaim the servant's exaltation and his significance for the world, while the chorus section concentrates on the servant's humiliation. The chorus itself is also dialogical, posing questions (53:1, 8) and alternatives (53:4–5) for discussion. The identity of the chorus is not explicated and may also, like the servant, be considered a tensive symbol: Is it Israel? the Gentile nations? us? An affirmative answer to all of these is warranted, always better with reference to a specific situation: the Exile, the Holocaust, Selma, Namibia, Cambodia.

The good news of God's vindication of the servant in the opening and closing speeches forms the brackets within which his humiliation is seen. It is precisely the one numbered with the transgressors who is the object of God's justification. The intent of 53:2–10 is to draw us into dialogue and thereby to have us recognize that God's justification is offered to those who are sinners—to those with whom the servant stands in solidarity.

Second Lesson: Heb. 4:14–16; 5:7–9. This pericope forms the brackets for the discussion of Jesus' qualifications as high priest on our behalf before the throne of God. It must be viewed within the greater context of Hebrews, with its rich description of the journey of the people of God toward their "rest," to the homeland God has prepared for them (11:13–14). The journey is fraught with temptations and perils, but God's people can have confidence (= *parrēsia*) because of the work of Jesus their High Priest.

Heb. 5:7–9 identifies the proper work of Jesus' high priesthood with his cross. Giver and gift, priest and victim are never separated before God's throne of grace, and only as such is Jesus "made perfect . . . the eternal source of salvation" (v. 9). Such perfection has communal scope in Hebrews (see the Second Lesson for Monday). As the source of salvation for God's people, as their source of grace in time of need, Jesus, victim and high priest, is made perfect.

That means that our drawing near to the throne of grace is never without the mediation of the Crucified (12:22–24). As in John's Gospel, the cross of Jesus is not the momentary victory of the forces of evil, the temporary defeat of God's Son; it is the place where the divine majesty is present, precisely the hour of glory. That is why the cross of Jesus calls the world's standards into question: to the world it seems to be the exact opposite of the hour of glory and the moment of salvation. It is, according to worldly standards, the sign of defeat, degradation, doubt, and despair.

It is therefore crucial to ground our interpretation of 4:14–16 in the work of the Crucified, that is, from the vantage point of 5:7–9. First of all, "through the heavens" signifies for the author not just the place of Jesus' reward but the arena of conflict. The "heavens" are the place of the worldly powers, or in Paul's words, the *stoicheia tou kosmou* (= the "elemental spirits of the universe"), which claim lordship and authority over us and to which we uncritically give our allegiance. The obedient one must suffer through them and die to them, because he does not belong to them. His death to them is victory over them.

Secondly, 4:15 must also be approached from the vantage point of 5:7–9, or interpretation may go far beyond the text. A high priest is our intercessor, one who stands in our stead. Who can best stand in for us but one who has stood where we stand? That Jesus is called a "great" High Priest signifies his uniqueness. He is our great High Priest because he faced the worldly powers and was tempted as we are; but instead of choosing their allure, instead of sinning, he overcame them through his obedience, by turning instead to God (5:7).

It is in connection with Jesus' cross that the author's words "yet without sinning" are related. The decision Jesus had to make on his way to the cross, depicted in all four Gospels (Mark 14:34ff., John 12:27ff.; cf. the Gospel for Tuesday), reminds us that he knows the power of our temptations and the allurement of the world's standards. He knows the power of sin, as well as our weaknesses in the face of it. But his decision was to face that power and not fall captive to it. By his act he broke the power of sin, not only for himself but for us: his act is complete as he becomes the source of our salvation, no longer as the humiliated one but as the exalted High Priest in our stead before the throne of God. With confidence, then, we face our own temptations, knowing that through our exalted High Priest we find mercy in time of weakness and grace to help in time of need.

Gospel: John 18:1—19:42. As stated in our treatment of the Gospels for Tuesday and Maundy Thursday we can speak of chap. 12 as a prelude to the Johannine passion narrative and chaps. 13—17 as Jesus' farewell discourses, actually the first act of the drama itself. The further events of the drama proper are recorded in John 18—19, which we shall review with an eye toward the special Johannine themes.

In John the suffering and death of Jesus are no longer an embarrassing problem for the church, no longer the momentary triumph of the forces of evil (cf. Luke 22:53), but the hour of Jesus' glory (see the Gospel for Tuesday) and the reason for which he had come (John 12:27). It is the victorious conclusion of the struggle of the light against the darkness. Therefore Jesus does not appear in the passion narrative so much as the Sufferer as the One who is in control of the events. Each step of the way he takes the initiative: in his trial (18:1–11), in the hearing before the high priest Annas (18:12–23), before Pilate (18:28—19:16). On the cross he provides for his mother (19:26–27), signals the conclusion of the drama in the context of God's plan (19:28), and dies with the knowledge that his work on earth is complete (19:30).

Therefore the cross is understood as the crowning conclusion to that which began with the Word made flesh (1:14). Of course, the resurrection of Jesus also belongs to the story. But the Risen One is identified and known precisely as the Crucified (20:27). The two are not to be separated, as is made clear throughout Jesus' ministry: he is the resurrection and the life (11:25; 14:16) and promises life to the one who believes in his word (5:24–25), because the Son has life in him as granted by the Father (5:26). In John's Gospel the event of the resurrection itself adds nothing to Jesus that he has not already possessed and is able to offer.

At the outset of the story of the arrest, 18:1–12, Jesus' control over the events is immediately established. He knows all that is about to happen to him (18:4) and takes the initiative straightway. His lordship is portrayed when the arresting band falls to the ground at his *ego eimi* (= "I am [he]," 18:6). Peter is identified as the one who reacts with swordplay and cuts off the right ear of the high priest's servant (leading some commentators to observe that Peter was left-handed, unless he struck a cowardly blow from behind!). There is no report of the disciples' flight, but it was alluded to already in 16:32; nor is there mention of Judas's kiss.

Jesus is led to a hearing before the high priest, identified as Annas, the father-in-law of the ruling high priest Caiaphas. V. 14 contains the purposeful ambiguity of a deeper meaning than the blindness of the political authorities can recognize (cf. 11:49–50). Jesus' reply to the high priest's interrogation in 18:20–21 serves to point out the farcical nature of the hearing, as does his response to the blow delivered by a servant of the high priest (18:22–23): both Annas and his servant appear absurd. Annas then sends Jesus bound to Caiaphas; there is no report of that hearing. The scene ends with Peter's denial and the fulfillment of Jesus' prediction of it in 13:38.

The report of the trial before Pilate (18:28—19:16a) is a unified account of a real trial; but it is more than a trial, it is a confrontation between the worldly power and the obedient Son of God, the representative of Caesar over against the Messiah-King. In 18:28–32, as Jesus is handed over to Pilate by the Jewish leadership, there is the ironic implication (v. 28) that the leadership meticulously holds fast to ceremonial prescriptions to avoid defilement while they lead to death the one whom God has sent! Their embarrassment is made more acute in the exchange between them and Pilate in vv. 30–32. Once again, what is being expressed here is not anti-Semitism but rather an intra-Jewish early Christian polemic against an institutional legalism which is blind to the very will of God it seeks to honor.

Pilate's interrogation of Jesus (18:33–38) shows the governor's conscientious investigation of whether the man before him might actually constitute a danger to the state. He proceeds on purely political grounds (v. 33). Jesus' answer (v. 34) makes Pilate admit that he has no reason of his own to proceed against Jesus but that he is feeling the pressure of the Jewish leadership (v. 35). That said, Jesus is then able to answer Pilate's original question; however, the answer is not really about himself but about his kingship: it is not of this world (v. 36). Pilate's reply fastens again on the person of Jesus: "So you are a king?" (v. 37). Jesus' answer is the familiar, purposely ambiguous answer which reverts the issue to the questioner: "You say that I am a king." Then follows a further explanation. As his kingship is eschatological, that is, from beyond this world and therefore not subject to the world's standards, so also is Jesus' origin from beyond the world. He has "come into the world" from beyond it "to bear witness to the truth" and does so here before the representative of worldly power. According to the world's standards, Pilate is Jesus' judge; but the actual fact of the matter is the reverse. But the world is not interested in truth (v. 38a).

Pilate's position, however, is not that of overt hostility but rather one of neutrality. The state can allow the preaching of the word to continue (v. 38b), even as it tries to avoid (by neutrality) the word's claims over against it. The state will attempt to find compromises (v. 39), but since it does not take the word seriously for itself, it is not strong enough to withstand the obstinate and unyielding demands of the world (v. 40). Without the word the state becomes afraid of the world and places itself at the world's disposal.

John 19:1–7 repeats this syndrome in Pilate's attempts at compromise and their rejection by the unbending crowd. His attempts to satisfy the world can serve to heighten his own anxiety (v. 8) and sink him more deeply into the world's control. The world plays upon Pilate's anxieties and uses them to secure its own ends (vv. 7–8, 12–13). Now Pilate must ask about Jesus' person (vv. 8–11); fearing the mysterious, he feels that his power may indeed be threatened if Jesus is indeed superhuman. "Where are you from?" Pilate asks; but Jesus remains silent, for no answer can be given which would resolve Pilate's anxiety or fading neutrality (v. 9). Pilate's crass reference to the power he has over Jesus extracts the comment from Jesus that whatever power Pilate has over him is given to him "from above" (v. 11). Pilate is the instrument through which God's plan is carried out. It is not on Pilate's initiative, however, that Jesus was handed over, but that of the Jewish leadership; therefore the latter has the greater sin (19:11b; with Bultmann we can understand the *ho paradous* of v. 11 in the light of 18:30; it does not refer to Judas or Caiaphas). But in attempting to compromise with the world, Pilate has compromised himself and lost his supposed neutrality; he will go against his own conviction, and therefore he too "has sin," even though not "the greater." Both he and the condemning crowd are without excuse.

In 19:12–16a (the first phrase of v. 17 in the English is v. 16b in the

Greek text), before Jesus is condemned to death, Pilate makes one last attempt to avoid the inevitable. The treatment of the soldiers (19:1–5) has made Jesus look powerless, even ridiculous; so he is brought out again and displayed before the crowd: can this defenseless figure be a threat to Caesar? (cf. 19:12). Pilate's question "Shall I crucify your king?" receives the shocking response "We have no king but Caesar." It is shocking, because by rejecting the Messiah God has sent, the crowd surrenders their eschatological hope. It has cut itself off from God's future. But a world at enmity with God is without hope, and by enacting its own designs rapidly moves toward self-destruction. Acceding to the crowd, Pilate delivers the Hope of Israel to death (v. 16).

It is as such Hope that Jesus is crucified (19:17–22), with Pilate's inscription providing his last act of insult and revenge on the crowd which had forced him to condemn Jesus. The irony continues, however, in that it is precisely as the Crucified that Jesus' kingship is realized; the cross is the exaltation of the Messiah (cf. 3:14–15; 8:28; 12:32); its time is the hour of his glory.

With the death of Jesus his work on earth is complete (19:28–30). Even here he takes the initiative, signaling the end with his final request (v. 28) in order "to fulfill the Scripture" (that is, Ps. 69:21). At the moment of his death, there is no loud cry (as in the synoptics), for Jesus dies not as the sufferer but as the King, who has successfully completed the work his Father gave him to do (10:18; 14:31; 17:4).

There is no parallel to 19:31–37 in the synoptic Gospels. The request to hasten the death of the crucified ones by breaking their legs is seen to be unnecessary in Jesus' case, since his death occurs on his own initiative. For security reasons a soldier lances Jesus' side, thereby fulfilling two prophecies (vv. 36–37). Once again, the Romans are not in control; they are only the instruments by which God's plan is carried out. From John's point of view the reference in v. 34b to the blood and water which flowed from the lance wound may signify that in the cross of Jesus the sacraments of baptism and the Lord's Supper have their foundation. The account of the burial in 19:38–42 includes Nicodemus along with Joseph of Arimathea as those who cared for Jesus' body, placing it in a new grave befitting a king. The narrative concludes simply and gently: "they laid Jesus there." There is no premonition of Easter.

In conclusion, the prospects for preaching in Holy Week on the lessons of cycle A, focusing on the Gospels of Matthew and John, are rich and promising. One last word should be said, however, as far as the figure of Pilate is concerned, namely that in the NT Gospels the tendency to exonerate Pilate and to place the blame on the Jews has already begun. Thus the second-century apocryphal Gospel of Peter has Herod, not Pilate, pronounce judgment on Jesus; the church father Tertullian held that Pilate was secretly a Christian *(Apology* 21); other legends claim that Pilate was martyred for Christ, and the Ethiopian church came to revere him as a saint. But there is no historical evidence whatsoever which would prevent the conclusion that Pontius Pilate was and remained anything other than a ruthless and vicious man, as ancient secular sources (and even Luke 13:1) describe him to have been. We must remember that the NT Gospels were written in a period of increasing hostility between church and synagogue, and certainly the Gospels of Matthew and John understand themselves as a part of an intra-Jewish religious conflict, far from an expression of gentile anti-Semitism. Therefore, our preaching on them, encouraged by cycle A, should guard against the use of Matthew and John to promote a racist hatred which in every way is repugnant to the texts and inconsistent with the teaching of the Lord to whom they bear witness.

HOMILETICAL INTERPRETATION

In his important book *God Was in Christ* (New York: Charles Scribner's Sons, 1948) Donald Baillie wrote, "Most of the great heresies arose from an undue desire for simplification, an undue impatience with mystery and paradox" (p. 107). As one reads the three lessons suggested for Good Friday in this lectionary series, one needs to resist the desire to reduce the story to some one interpretation, to ease the mystery and resolve the paradox. It may be rather our responsibility and our joy to add to it—add ourselves and our gifts and our culture and our time.

Of course, we cannot "add" to the gospel, but when we make it our own, when we bring our life and times within its embrace, we add to its domain. This appropriation of the gospel and its subsequent expression in Christianity in many times and places is part of its richness. The Rev. John S. Mbiti, professor of theology at Makere Union College in Uganda, asks: "Are we to inherit a largely bankrupt Christianity from the west, and cherish it in our bosoms without adding anything to it? I believe that some enrichment can come to Christianity from our African background. We can add nothing to the Gospel for this is an eternal gift of God; but Christianity is always a beggar seeking food and drink, cover and shelter from the cultures and times it encounters in its never-ending journeys and wanderings" ("Christianity & Traditional Religions in Africa," *International Re-*

view of Mission, October 1970, p. 438). We began the week with the very long "Story of the Death of Jesus" in Matthew, and we end it with an equally long "Story of the Death of Jesus" in the Fourth Gospel. It is the same story but it is told in a very different way. The "cover and shelter" provided is different, and it encourages us to take the story into our time and our life too. Perhaps that is what being a Christian is all about. The preacher working with these texts will do well not to presume too much, not to be dogmatic, but to encourage persons to listen and respond from within their own "cover and shelter," that the gospel may be received there.

If we begin with the narrative from John, we may find that simply to read it is enough for the day's proclamation. Or we may wish to lift up some particular part of it. The preacher is well advised to respect his or her own response as possibly a prompting of the Holy Spirit. Thus it may be wise to stop and ponder the verse or scene or idea which reaches out and touches you in surprise as you read and makes you exclaim inwardly, "I never saw that before!" The exegesis helps us to find many points of interest or explore ones which rise up in our reading: Jesus as the one in charge of the events, dominating the scenes before Annas and before Pilate; Jesus providing for his mother, completing his work; the personal drama which swirls around Pilate, the representative of the state; the contrast between the "power" of the defenseless figure of Jesus and the imperial power of Rome.

The preacher may provoke intense curiosity by noting the interruption of this passion narrative by what seems entirely insignificant: a report about the time of day (19:14). This evangelist pauses to tell us that it is twelve o'clock noon on the day before Passover. Is there something important about that time? When the interpreter tracks down that seemingly casual reference, he uncovers the Passover theme again and learns that it occurs three times in John's Gospel.

The first time (2:13–25) Jesus cleanses the temple. Bible scholars suggest he is substituting his own body for the temple. In Jesus' second encounter with the Passover (6:4) he doesn't go to Jerusalem. Why should he? He has already substituted himself. He goes to the wilderness, and it becomes the occasion for the discourse on the Bread of Life. May we say that he substitutes himself for the Passover meal? (Here is another connection to the Exodus.) Then we come to this Good Friday passage and the strange interruption we have noted when the evangelist gives us the time of day as though we had dialed the telephone company for that information. So what is important about that? Are we helped to think of the sun high in the sky or of Pilate growing restless for his noonday meal? But more is there: this is the time when priests begin to slaughter animals for the next day. So now, for the fourth evangelist, may we say that Jesus becomes the Passover victim, who bears the Sin (capital S) of the entire cosmos? See then how this could tie in with the First Lesson for the day.

Here is action, and we may remember that early in Holy Week the preacher helped us understand that we know *person* best by action, an identifiable pattern of action. The Bible presents that action in history and in nature and supremely in a human being (Eller, *His End Up,* pp. 58–60):

> Some ancient Hebrews listened carefully to their history. . . and. . . they heard not the unarranged smash and clatter that most men hear; within their history they heard a melody, a person-melody. . . . Some of the dominant notes were grace, promise, law, redemption, covenant, lordship. . . . it should be considered that the notes we have named are free, purposed, relational, presentative actions all—precisely what we [have] defined as constituting *person*-pattern. . . . the melody heard in their history was that of a Person par excellence. . . .
>
> Then there lived a man; and one day his followers turned to one another and said, "Listen! Listen to that man! Not only is his a real great *person*-melody [it is the same one we have heard before. . . in our history. . . in nature, free, purposed, relational, presentative]. Listen to it loud, clear, and sweet—easier even for human ears to follow than by listening to history." With these followers, this is the conviction we express when we speak of God the Son. God the Son is God's person-pattern as perceived through the "natural" carrier of the human body of Jesus of Nazareth.

Herman Waetjen suggests that the title Son of man is the most important statement of the nature of Jesus, a christological statement (and that is what the Good Friday proclamation is!). He suggests it be translated in our time, in our "cover and shelter" (to use the Ugandan Christian's words), as "the new human being," "the human being par excellence." He is the "new human being" in whom the image of God is restored. If ever the task and vocation of the Christian pulpit is "the showing forth" of this new human being, it is in the Good Friday event.

An Orthodox priest, speaking at the Notre Dame conference on Vatican II, addressed a question to the Roman Catholic Church which may well be addressed to all of us who are so preoccupied with determination to make Christ "relevant" to secular life that it begins to seem as though it is Christ who must conform. Father John Meyendorff asked if the "Roman Church [is] always right in its traditional preoccupation . . . to find solutions to all human problems, to guide, to feed, to advise, to rule and to direct instead of showing." It is this "showing forth," within and from our "cover and shelter," our finitude, which is our task especially on Good Friday.

James Stewart of Edinburgh spoke of Good Friday when he delivered the Lyman Beecher Lectures. He reminded us of the synoptic tradition about the veil of the temple being rent from top to bottom (*A Faith to Proclaim* [London: Hodder & Stoughton, 1953], pp. 80–81):

> The veil had been hanging there for years. It looked as though it might hang there forever. . . . It was there to fulfil a double function. On the one hand, it was there to keep men out: a warning to sinful man that where the last mysteries of religion were concerned he must keep a respectful distance. On the other hand, it was there to shut God in; for behind that hanging veil there was silence deep as death and darkness black as night, even while the sun was blazing outside. It had been hanging there for years: it looked as if it might hang there forever. . . .
>
> This was Judaism's *deus absconditus*. This was the perpetual frustration of man's search for the eternal. But one day Jesus died; and from top to bottom . . . the veil was rent. Here was the decisive revelatory event: man's agelong fumbling quest was at an end.

"The Story of the Death of Jesus" as told by the fourth evangelist is appropriately framed in this lectionary by the fourth servant song from Isaiah and the magnificent "great High Priest" passage from Hebrews. The exegesis has sensitively directed us to take guard against identifying the servant with only one figure in history. Yet because we do identify the servant with that one figure so fundamentally, all servants come into their own. So also with the Priest, although there is no question of his identification. Because Jesus of Nazareth, crucified and risen, is Servant and Priest, all the John Ashleys of the universe, from Uganda to Iowa, from the first century to the twenty-first, do not walk alone down the long road from their first freedom to their final freedom. Alongside them, ahead of them and behind them, is One who has been in every respect tempted as they and who gives them confidence to draw near to the throne of grace.